How Can We Believe?

ROBERT J. DEAN
HOW CAN WE BELIEVE?

BROADMAN PRESS
NASHVILLE, TENNESSEE

© Copyright 1978 • Broadman Press.

All rights reserved.

4281-35

ISBN: 0-8054-8135-4

Dewey Decimal Classification: 239

Subject Heading: APOLOGETICS

Library of Congress Catalog Card Number: 77-87248

Printed in the United States of America

Dedicated

to

Betty

INTRODUCTION

A young pastor announced a series of sermons on reasons for Christian faith. He was fresh from a situation in which he had been forced to defend and explain his faith to many who denied the truth of what he believed. After listening to his sermon on reasons for faith in God, one loyal member of the congregation said: "Pastor, no matter what you say, I still believe in God!"

Her experiences had been different from those of her pastor. She had never known many people who did not share her basic beliefs and values. Therefore, her pastor's attempts to answer arguments against the Christian faith exposed her for the first time to those arguments. And although the pastor was seeking to refute those arguments, she considered any mention of the arguments as an attack on her faith.

There are people like her, people who have never faced the challenges of an unbelieving society—at least not personally. But such Christians are becoming fewer and fewer. The reasons are obvious: Unbelievers are becoming more numerous and more vocal. Their views are given ever-widening ranges of influence. More and more people are exposed to views of knowledge that question all the presuppositions of Christian faith. Therefore, in an age of growing unbelief, Christians need more than ever to be able to offer a reasonable explanation and defense of their faith.

The words of 1 Peter 3:15 surely apply to this generation of

Christian believers: "Always be prepared to make a defense to any one who calls you to account for the hope that is in you, yet do it with gentleness and reverence."

This book is written for two groups of people: It is written, first of all, for Christian believers who are aware of the challenge of understanding and explaining their faith. It also is written for unbelievers who sometimes wonder *How can Christians believe that?* and perhaps at times also wonder *How can I believe?* A dogmatic unbeliever is not likely to listen to reasons for Christian faith, but a wistful unbeliever may.

The six chapters probe aspects of the larger question: How can we believe—(1) in God in an age of science? (2) in a God of love when there is so much suffering? (3) what the New Testament says about Jesus? (4) that Christ offers what we really need? (5) that God really answers prayer? (6) in life after death?

Many readers will recognize that this approach is what theologians call *Christian apologetics*. The original meaning of "apology" is different from the prevailing modern meaning. The original meaning of the word is a defense. The goal of Christian apologetics is to defend and explain what Christians believe and why.

There are several schools of thought about the proper approach to take in defending and explaining the faith. At one extreme are those who believe that a strong case for Christianity can be made on purely rational grounds. In its most extreme form this approach almost does away with the need for faith. Reason becomes the primary means of leading people to God; faith becomes intellectual assent to almost irresistible conclusions of rational arguments.

At the other extreme are those who question whether reason has any value in inducing or encouraging Christian faith. Faith is not intellectual assent but personal commitment and trust. God is not found at the end of a rational argument, but by a commitment which in many ways is like a leap in the dark. Christ and the way of the cross, although paradoxically true to life's deepest realities,

Introduction

run counter to the usual processes of human reasoning.

Both positions contain some truth. Faith is basically a commitment, not intellectual assent to a series of propositions. And Christ and the way of the cross seem as intellectually scandalous to many people today as they did to many in the first century (see 1 Cor. 1:18–25). However, Christian faith is not exercised in a vacuum. It is not blind gullibility that flies in the face of reality. There are evidences that tend to validate Christian faith; there are reasons that help to explain it.

Elton Trueblood makes a strong case for an approach to apologetics that he calls "rational Christianity." He maintains that attention must be given to the intellectual content of Christian faith. He is well aware of the fallacy of those systems that almost reduce Christianity to a series of propositions and rational proofs. However, anti-intellectualism is an overreaction that is equally false and dangerous. What is needed is an approach that gives proper attention to all three essential aspects of living Christian faith: the inner life of devotion, the intellectual life of rational thought, and the outer life of human service.[1]

Such rational Christianity enables Christians to come to a high degree of certainty about the foundations of their faith. If a person does not consider the intellectual basis for his faith, he is bound to be plagued at times by nagging fears that he is building on shifting sands. But a person of genuine commitment who honestly examines the rational content of his faith can hold to his faith with full intellectual integrity amid all the modern currents of intellectual life. Likewise, he can effectively set forth the claims of his faith to others, even those who are unbelievers.

Unless otherwise noted, all Scripture verses are taken from the Revised Standard Version of the Bible.

All Scripture verses marked KJV are taken from the King James Version.

CONTENTS

Introduction   vii

1.
How Can We Believe in God in an
Age of Science?   13

2.
How Can We Believe in a God of Love
When There Is So Much Suffering?   30

3.
How Can We Believe What the New Testament
Says About Jesus?   43

4.
How Can We Believe that Christ Offers
What We Really Need?   62

5.
How Can We Believe that God Really
Answers Prayer?   83

6.
How Can We Believe in Life After Death?   102

1
How Can We Believe in God in an Age of Science?

In the early sixties the United States was behind in the race for space. On August 6–7, 1961 the Russian cosmonaut Gherman S. Titov orbited the earth seventeen times in twenty-five hours. He was the second Russian to orbit the earth. The Russians gloated over their achievements. The American scientific community winced and squirmed at the exploits of Titov and his fellow cosmonaut Yuri Gagarin.

Titov proved to be a very talkative celebrity. He was interviewed many times and gave his views on many subjects. He could not resist venturing into the field of religion. He claimed that his space flight had verified the atheistic view that there is no God. After all, Titov pointed out, he had been in the heavens and he had not seen God or any evidence of God.

By contrast, the first three humans to orbit the moon bore witness to their faith in God. The astronauts of Apollo 8—Frank Borman, James Lovell, and William Anders—concluded their televised 1968 Christmas Eve message to earth by reading Genesis 1:1–10, which begins, "In the beginning God created the heaven and the earth." Each man read some of the verses from this beginning passage in the Bible. The public reaction to this reading was mixed. Many applauded it as highly appropriate; others were critical of this public display of religion in connection with the Apollo program. The Soviets seemed puzzled. Their radio comment was: "It would be interesting to know what this means. Is it a joke or a space attempt to strengthen the authority of religion which has been shaken by the flight itself?"

How can this be? How can a believer and an unbeliever see the same thing and each see it as evidence to support his own position? Any serious attempt to answer this question must come to grips with the central issues in why some people believe in God and others do not.

Is Faith Blind?

Ours has been called an age of unbelief. Many people have serious difficulties with the idea of believing in God. Some call themselves atheists because they deny the existence of God. Others prefer to be called agnostics. They do not say, "There is no God"; instead, they say, "We do not know whether or not God exists." Another group of unbelievers goes farther than traditional atheists or agnostics. This group, called logical positivists, considers any discussion of the subject to be a waste of time. Their position is that any language or statements about God are unprovable, therefore, only nonsense.

One basic assumption is held by all these different kinds of unbelievers: The age of science has put an end to faith in God. The atheist maintains that the evidence of science is strong enough to prove there is no God. The agnostic is not willing to be so dogmatic, but he refuses to believe in a God who cannot be proved scientifically.

A group of army officers were discussing religion. One man said: "I was raised on the scientific method, and no one has ever been able to prove to me scientifically that God exists." As he spoke, he noticed a chaplain joining the group. The skeptic explained that he had intended no disrespect.

"It's quite all right," the chaplain said. "As a matter of fact, your problem is similar to one of my own. I was raised on the theological method, and no one has ever been able to prove to me theologically that an atom exists."

"But whoever heard of finding an atom by theology?" the skeptic protested.

"Exactly," agreed the chaplain.

A college student told his pastor that he had had his eyes opened about the fantasy of faith in God. The pastor asked him what he thought faith was. The student said: "It is believing the unbelievable, accepting something for which there is no proof. It is a blind leap in the dark, an act of sheer superstition."

The pastor challenged this definition. He said: "Faith in God is based on evidence as surely as science is; the difference is in the kinds of evidence on which each is based." The pastor took a rose and said: "The rose is red. That is a statement for which there is scientific evidence. But suppose I say, 'The rose is beautiful.' That statement cannot be tested scientifically, but is it not still true?"

These stories illustrate a basic problem: Persons with different presuppositions have difficulty communicating. Our presuppositions are reflected in the words we use and how we use them. The same word can mean different things to different people. Words like *faith, proof,* and *evidence* do not mean the same thing to the field of scientific studies as they do in the area of religion. As a result, basic problems of communication hinder any attempt by Christians to explain their faith to persons who have completely different presuppositions about the meaning of key words.

As already noted, logical positivists refuse to admit that religious language is anything more than nonsense. Many modern philosophers are more tolerant: they are willing to concede that theological language is meaningful in expressing distinctively religious convictions, feelings, and presuppositions. If we are serious about communicating, we need to be aware of the context out of which we speak and the context out of which others hear what we say.[1]

The skeptical army officer and the college student were speaking out of a different set of presuppositions than the chaplain and the pastor. The chaplain and the pastor were trying to make their protagonists aware of the two different sets of presuppositions. They also were hoping to open the minds of the officer and the student to the validity of a set of presuppositions that is not rooted in the context and terminology of science.

Many who do not believe in God tend to assume that their own position is based on solid, objective evidence. They also assume that people who have faith in God are only exercising blind, gullible superstition. In other words, they use the words *prove* and *evidence* of their own position; and they attribute the Christian's position to *faith*, which they define in their own way as blind superstition. A simplistic caricature contrasts an open-minded scientist in search of the truth with a close-minded believer with his determination to believe in God in spite of all the evidence. This caricature is not accurate.

For one thing, *everyone* has certain basic presuppositions, which represent a kind of faith. The scientist, for example, seeks to approach his task with an open mind, but he also brings to his task certain basic assumptions and from time to time certain intuitive insights. Eric Rust, who is trained in both science and theology, points out that in this sense science proceeds on the basis of faith: "The scientist is a committed man, and his approach to nature is guided by the presuppositions that underlie his thought. He believes in a rational structure in the universe, a 'hidden' which is there for him to discover, a 'hidden' which is also given to him and open to his investigation." [2]

When we move beyond the physical sciences, the presuppositions become even more apparent. The irony of this "faith" is especially evident in the case of the logical positivists, who so dogmatically rule out any statement of religious language. The logical positivists judge everything by this basic proposition: "No statement of fact is meaningful unless it can be verified in sense experience." The irony is that this basic proposition cannot be verified in sense experience and, judged by itself, is meaningless. Thus the logical positivist begins with an act of faith that his basic premise is true.[3]

Another striking example of secular faith is the belief of naturalistic humanism that humanity can create a brave new world. Communism is an extreme example of this point of view. God and religion are rejected in favor of humanity's unaided ability to make a happy, fruitful world. Yet the basic premise of this view is itself an act of faith—faith in humanity's ability to create a utopia.

Thus everyone operates on the principle of faith in certain basic areas of life. The believer in God is not unique in this respect. However, he is honest enough to acknowledge that the basic premise of his living is an act of faith—in his case, faith in God. He is willing to admit that God cannot be proved scientifically; on the other hand, he rejects the notion that his faith is blind and irrational.

The word *proof* or *prove*, like the word *faith*, is another key word in the whole discussion. There was a time when believers sought to prove God with certain logical arguments. The basic fallacy with the classic "proofs" of God is that no faith would be required if there were absolute proof. We cannot prove God either with scientific tests or logical arguments. God is no more found at the end of a logical argument than he is with a test tube and microscope. Believing in God is an act of faith.

However, this faith is not a blind, unreasonable act. God is not found at the end of logical argument, but there are logical reasons for believing in God. There is no absolute proof for God, but there is convincing evidence to encourage those who believe in God.

When a Christian says or writes, "God cannot be proved," his meaning often is misunderstood. The average person may understand this to mean that there is no convincing evidence for God's existence. The average modern person also may quickly contrast this "unfounded" religious belief with the "proven" results of scientific knowledge. He is wrong on both counts. The notion of *absolute* proof in any area is a false assumption; what we do have is the possibility of high degrees of probability based on cumulative evidence. Elton Trueblood points out that this principle "applies not only to evidence for the existence of God, but also to evidence for the existence of atoms and to evidence for the existence of historical characters." [4]

A true scientist does not claim absolute proof for some position. However, he does accept something as true if the evidence strongly supports it. The Christian believes that there is strong evidence to support his faith in God. The word *evidence* is crucial. What is evidence? The word has a specialized meaning to a scientist. He may have trouble accepting as evidence what the believer sets forth as evidence of God. If he rigidly demands that only a certain kind of evidence is valid, he is making an unfair demand. If God is real, he is not the kind of reality one finds by restricting the evidence to only one kind. A truly scientific approach tries to be open to all possible evidence. An open-minded person does not prejudge the conclusion by ruling out the evidence before it is heard.

The rest of this chapter will examine three converging lines of evidence that support the claim for a high degree of probability for faith in God. Within themselves these lines of evidence do not produce faith. Two people can consider the same claims: one may believe and the other may not. Faith does not operate in a vacuum, but faith always has a personal dimension—a willingness to exercise trust and commitment. Those who believe in God, therefore, should find their faith strengthened by these lines of evidence. Those who do not believe may not be convinced to take the leap of faith; but hopefully they will at least see that faith in God is not a blind, gullible act of sheer superstition.

Look at the Universe

When the three Americans orbited the moon, they saw the earth from a new perspective. As they sought a way to convey their feelings, they decided to read the biblical account of creation. Their new perspective tended to reaffirm their faith in God as Creator. Their feelings, however, were little different from the feelings of believers in every age who have seen evidences of God's hand in his creation. Centuries ago a believer wrote:

> The heavens are telling the glory of God;
> and the firmament proclaims his handiwork (Ps. 19:1).

If God is indeed the Creator of the heavens and the earth, it is reasonable to assume that we can see reflections of the Creator in the creation. To the eyes of faith, many things testify to the Creator's handiwork—the beauty we see, the orderliness of nature, the awesome magnitude of the universe.

The rise of modern science seemed to pose a threat to religious faith. Science proposed natural explanations to many areas that previously had been shrouded in mystery. Science seemed to be denying the hand of a divine Creator. George A. Buttrick writes: "Indeed there were scientists, in the fearsome days of the mechanists, who frankly gave the impression that they had conducted God to the edge of His universe and summarily dismissed Him." [5] A vicious war of words broke out between advocates of science and defenders of religion. Many scientists and many believers now regret that period of history. They realize now that science and religion are complementary, not contradictory.

Wernher von Braun, who led in developing America's rocket program, said: "I regard the Creator and His creation as an entity . . . . To me, science and religion are like two windows in a house through which we look at the reality of the Creator and the laws manifested in His creation." [6]

Science and religion are complementary because they provide

two perspectives with which to view the universe. Each perspective is needed to take account of all the phenomena and to provide an adequate overall view of reality. Science seeks to answer the *when* and *how* questions about the universe; religion addresses the *who* and *why* questions. Science legitimately examines the observable data of the universe and seeks to unlock the secrets of how the universe is put together and how it functions. By contrast, the first two chapters of Genesis were not written as a scientific handbook on the universe. Rather, these chapters affirm God as Creator and point toward his purpose in creating. The rest of the Bible elaborates on that purpose.

The crucial question is this: Is an intelligent purpose responsible for the universe? Some scientists and philosophers assume that nature is a closed, naturalistic system: everything has a purely natural explanation; the universe is a purely natural phenomenon. Other scientists and philosophers, however, see evidences of intelligent purpose in the universe. They believe that the universe makes sense only if we assume mind and purpose in nature. This assumption is thoroughly consistent with the biblical teaching that God created the universe.

The evidence is not so conclusive as to prove or disprove an intelligent purpose in the universe. The universe seems a strange mixture of purpose and purposelessness. Thus a person's view on this issue depends on his basic presuppositions. Each side can cite evidence to support its position. Therefore, those who believe in God as Creator do not base their case on conclusive proof. Rather, believers maintain that there is enough evidence of mind and purpose in nature to make this a reasonable probability.

The debate usually centers around the meaning of human life and intelligence. No one denies that intelligent life is a part of the natural order. Human beings have minds. The question is, "Where did these minds come from?" One school of thought maintains that human intelligence is a purely natural phenomenon that has evolved of itself. According to this view, human life and intelligence is only a kind of accident of nature that has occurred in a remote part of a vast, unthinking universe. Others, however, point out that the emergence of intelligent life presupposes some Mind back of the process. William Temple's words point to the reasonableness of the latter conclusion: *"The more completely we include Mind within Nature, the more inexplicable must Nature become except by reference to Mind."* [7]

Mind and purpose go together. Eric Rust points out that the physical sciences have tried to avoid any consideration of purpose. They have been more successful in this than the sciences that deal with human life. The attempts to rule out any concepts of purpose from biology and psychology have been unsuccessful.[8]

Causes and results of natural phenomena are in the realm of scientific explanation, but what about the larger purpose that gives overall meaning to the phenomena? This purpose, if it can be perceived, provides an explanation on a deeper level than the scientific explanations of secondary causes. Elton Trueblood uses the analogy of a carpenter driving a nail:

> The nail goes in *because* the hammer hits it. The hammer head moves *because* it is moved by the muscles of a man's arm. The arm muscles move *because* they are directed by the nerve impulses. But the whole enterprise takes place *because* a man has a reason for driving a nail in a board . . . . Our ordinary language obscures the true situation in that we use the same word 'because' in each case, but reflection shows that the word in its fourth use means something very different from what it means in the first three uses. The first three do not really explain, but the fourth *does* explain.[9]

The language of religious faith is able to speak of that kind of explanation that grows out of purpose. This is the reason scientific explanations of *when* and *how* need to be complemented by religious explanations of *who* and *why*.

I have tried not to claim more from this line of evidence than is justified. However, it is difficult to exercise restraint when considering the alternatives: a wholly naturalistic explanation of the universe or an explanation that includes faith in God. Earlier I wrote of "reasonable probability." Some may feel that this is too strong. Personally I feel it is not strong enough when the alternatives are considered.

A purely naturalistic explanation must assume that the universe just happened. This assumption requires an act of faith at least as great as the assumption that intelligent purpose lies back of the universe. Given a choice between believing that God created the universe and believing that it all just happened, I prefer to believe that God is Creator. Personally, this requires less "blind" faith than believing that it all is the result of the interaction of purely natural forces.

And I need to add this other personal word: Faith in God is not only a more believable alternative but also a much more satisfying one. This faith gives some meaning to the universe, which otherwise would be empty and meaningless. George Buttrick writes, "We must live 'as if,' as if the Universe were nonsense or as if it were mere cold law, or as if it was a Father's House." [10] Given this choice—and this is the choice we are given—many of us prefer to live as if it is the Father's house.

Look at Human Beings

The Bible teaches that God made man in his own image. If this is true, we can reasonably assume that we can see something of God not only in the universe as a whole but also in humankind in particular. We already have noted that man's mind suggests the divine mind. People of faith also believe that humans have a moral and a spiritual nature that reflects our Creator.

Since the time of Immanuel Kant, the moral argument for God has been used to testify to the reasonableness of faith in God. Elton

Trueblood developed this line of thought in his book *Philosophy of Religion*. He maintains that a sense of moral obligation is a part of the human experience. Human beings struggle with a sense of oughtness.[11] Trueblood believes that this sense of oughtness is meaningless unless there is an objective moral order. Anthropologists often stress the differing moral standards that characterize people of different cultures. The differences are real, but they should not blind us to

> a significant agreement in moral convictions, an agreement too great to be accounted for by coincidence . . . . In our reaction against the provincialism of our earlier moral ideas we have tended to exaggerate the differences in moral judgment which appear in different cultures. What exists is neither full agreement nor absolute confusion, but *authentic development*, roughly parallel to what we observe in a scientific development from magic to modern science. At a high level of competence the agreement among moralists is very striking.[12]

How are we to account for this objective moral order? Why is it that intelligent people of all ages and cultures have such wide areas of agreement about what people ought to do? There is more than one possible answer to these questions, but by far the most reasonable explanation for an objective moral order is God. "The mystery of life is always great, but if there is a moral order and yet no divine Mind as the locus of that order, the mystery is impenetrable indeed."[13]

When C. S. Lewis was an atheist, he raged against God because his own sense of kindness and justice was offended by much he saw in nature and human society. He argued that a good God could not have made and presided over such a world. Then Lewis began to wonder at the source of his own concern for love and justice. Years later, after he had become a Christian, he wrote: "My argument against God was that the universe seemed so cruel and unjust. But how had I got this idea of *just* and *unjust*? A man does not call a line crooked unless he has some idea of a straight line. What was I comparing this universe with when I called it unjust?" [14] This line of argument caused one of the cracks in the carefully built foundation of his unbelief. The most reasonable explanation for his own sense of justice was a God of justice.

Thus mankind's moral nature testifies to God. Is that not also true of humanity's spiritual nature, which is reflected in religious experience? Again Elton Trueblood sets forth the evidence in a compelling way.[15] He points out four undeniable facts: (1) Millions of people throughout human history have testified to a personal encounter with God. (2) The character of many of the reporters is unquestionably trustworthy in other areas; therefore, they are presumably trustworthy in this area also. (3) There are strong areas of agreement running through these testimonies. That is, the witnesses describe what happened to them in ways similar to those others describe what happened to them. (4) In many cases there was a noticeable and lasting change in their lives.

Critics try to discount the validity of this kind of evidence. One popular criticism is to say that a religious experience is not valid evidence because it is not based on sensory perceptions. Yet this objection overlooks the strong and compelling nature of the evidence. Is it reasonable to assume that this many people would testify to a relatively similar experience unless there was some reality involved?

Another popular criticism is to discount religious experience on the basis of one's own failure to have had such an experience. Trueblood tells of a physiologist who asserted that he did not believe in God and that he had never had any sense of the presence of God in his life. Trueblood comments:

> Here was a highly intelligent person with a finely trained mind, and the negative evidence provided by his testimony must be given considerable weight. But wait a moment! Are we so sure?

> Before we give this testimony *any weight at all* we need to know much more. Did the scholar in question submit himself to the kind of situation in which he could expect to be aware of God's presence, if God really is?[16]

By contrast, Leslie Weatherhead recorded this testimony given by a scientist whom he heard lecture at Cambridge:

> My father and mother were deeply religious. My brother and I had no time for religion. We thought that religion was all right for old people, but we were scientists and we thought we had found our way through by what we were pleased to call scientific methods. Then my brother was killed. My father and mother had resources, and with their resources they could meet that shattering loss. But I had no one. I had no resources at all. One night, broken-hearted and with all my proud science in ruined uselessness at my feet, I knelt down. I did not know how to pray. I had scorned prayer, but I put out my hand *and I found it was grasped.* I knew that Someone was coming to my help and somehow I knew it was Christ.[17]

(This testimony is stated in uniquely Christian terms. Not all who testify to religious experiences do so in Christian terminology. Chapter 4 will deal in more detail with the uniquely Christian claims about religious experience.)

Look at History

The Bible writers saw God's hand in the events of their history. They were not philosophers who came to believe in God because of convincing arguments for his existence. Rather, they were witnesses who testified to God's activity in history and in their own lives.

The Bible itself is a record of those who bore witness to God's revelation in history. The genius of biblical revelation is not a series of propositions or statements about God, but testimonies to God's actions in human history. The Old Testament is the prophetic witness to God's actions in the history of Israel. The New

Testament is the apostolic witness to God's work in Jesus Christ.

The Old Testament at times—as in Psalm 19:1—testifies to God's revelation in nature. However, over and over again the Old Testament tells of God's revelation in the experience of Israel. The heart of this revelation was the Exodus. The Hebrews never called this an escape; rather, they viewed it as a divine deliverance. They were hopelessly enslaved by one of the superpowers of the day. They cried for deliverance; but when deliverance came, they often held back. Even their leader Moses had been reluctant to accept the divine leading. Thus the Exodus became for Israel clear evidence of God's redemptive power and concern on their behalf. Later writers referred back to the Exodus and interpreted events in their day as God's continued leadership.

Likewise, the New Testament testifies to God's activity in history—in this case his redemptive power and concern in Jesus Christ. His coming, his life, his death, his resurrection are seen as God's supreme revealing and redeeming activity in human history. Chapter 3 will deal at more length with this central feature of Christian faith. However, at this point we do need to emphasize that Christians consider Jesus Christ as the center of history and the focal point of their faith. The biblical witnesses did not reason their way to God on the basis of evidences in nature or in man; rather, they responded to what they believed to be God's activity in history. They assumed God at work at many points in history, but they viewed Jesus Christ as the focal point that provides the clue to understanding creation, history, and human existence.[18]

Two important questions must be asked: (1) Did these biblical events actually happen? (2) Do these events testify to activity by God? The first question probes the trustworthiness of the Bible. The overall accuracy has been vindicated again and again by discoveries from the past. Yet as in the case of God so in the case of the Bible, there is a sense in which faith is the crucial issue. A person either accepts the Bible as trustworthy and authoritative, or he does not accept it. Again, however, as in the case of God so also in the case of the Bible, this faith is not blind gullibility. There is solid evidence that the Bible is a trustworthy authority.

Several years ago a skeptic offered to pay a certain amount of money to any believer who could prove to him that such a person as Jesus ever lived. The key words, of course, are "prove to him." The skeptic knew he was safe from having to pay off. He had already decided that no amount of evidence would prove this to him.

One wonders whether the skeptic believes in the reality of anyone in history. How about Julius Caesar? or Christopher Columbus? or George Washington? We assume that such people lived because of the records of their day and because of their impact on history since then. How much more is this true of Jesus? Of course, not all the factual data in the Bible has made such an impact as Jesus Christ; however, history bears the marks and lasting impression of the major events recorded in the Bible.

Even if we accept the events as historical, the second question remains: Do these events testify to activity by God? Skeptics argue that there are other possible explanations of these events. Believers maintain that the Bible's explanation for these events makes more sense than any other proposal.

In earlier generations some historians spoke of writing a purely objective account of human history. This so-called "scientific" approach to history would grow out of the facts of history itself, not out of any preconceptions of the historian. Most historians now recognize that such a goal is unrealistic. All of us, including historians, have basic premises from which we operate. Every historian writes from some point of view. This is the basis on which he decides what to include in his history and how to explain what he includes. His perspective guides him in selecting certain pivotal events and personalities from a vast number of items that are possibilities for inclusion. The historian is not driven to some one point of view as the only explanation of the facts. He knows that other interpretations are possible, but he believes that his own interpretation fits more of the facts and makes more sense of them.

Thus the biblical writers were not the only persons to interpret historical events from a point of view. They wrote from the perspective of faith, but they did not force events to fit into an arbitrarily preconceived mold. Rather, the pattern of the events they interpreted fits the shape of their principle of interpretation. Modern believers share their perspective. We recognize that other interpretations of biblical events are possible; however, we believe that subsequent history tends to vindicate the Bible writers. Their explanation for the Exodus and for Jesus Christ fits more of the data than any other explanation. Likewise, the continued impact of these crucial events testifies to the hand of God both then and now. Either history is meaningless, or it has some purpose and direction. We believe that it has purpose and that divine activity is the clue to that purpose.

Believing Is Seeing

We are accustomed to saying "seeing is believing," but there is a sense in which "believing is seeing." Faith in God is not, as many unbelievers assume, an act of blind trust with no rational basis. On the other hand, faith in God does call for *faith*. The three lines of evidence noted in this chapter support a reasonable probability for God, but the evidence does not provide absolute proof. Faith is essential in order to know God. Faith is much more than intellectual assent to some proposition about God; faith is personal commitment that is expressed in prayer, trust, worship, and service.

The experience of commitment to God opens the way to a wider scope of insight than an intellectual seeker ever can know. The best advice to an open-minded person, therefore, is to exercise what faith you have—however small. Horace Bushnell was once so filled with skepticism that he believed nothing beyond the fact that right is right. So he prayed to the abstract principle of right. Yet this honest prayer led toward growing light and faith. He prayed in the same spirit as did the man in the Bible who said, "I believe; help my unbelief" (Mark 9:24). God hears and answers such a prayer.

Many people try to adopt a neutral position on the question of God. This agnostic position is attractive because it seems so scientific: "I don't know whether or not God is real; I'm waiting until the evidence either proves or disproves God." Actually this is a kind of cop-out, for no one discovers whether or not God is real by waiting for God to be proved to him. There are converging lines of evidence, but a person does not come to God without exercising some faith. Those who take literally the motto "seeing is believing" never see some of life's deepest realities. These realities become real to the eyes of faith. Such faith calls for courage and commitment. It is risky, but the way of bland agnosticism also is risky, in a different way.

George A. Buttrick puts it this way:

> Life waits upon this venture of faith as Jesus constantly declared. Our modern demand "Prove it to me," easily becomes cowardice. This kind of mind sits at home to receive all arguments about God. The gravedigger, the mystic, the novelist, and the chemist call in turn. This prove-it-to-me mind is scientifically polite to all, and serves afternoon tea. When the guests have gone it ponders the arguments, and concludes: "I find no convincing proof; I am an agnostic . . . ." The defect of the proof-demanding mind is that it can never reach any conclusion. It can never reach anything, because it does not move. It just sits, and waits for certainties . . . . It cannot strongly believe or disbelieve, for it is noncommittal, and may therefore end by being trivial. The apparent equipoise of life is tipped to the side of *certitude*—not necessarily *certainty*—only by the courage of faith.[19]

2
How Can We Believe in a God of Love When There Is So Much Suffering?

Leonard Griffith tells of a woman who said to a minister: "We have had nothing but tragedy in our home. Mother died of cancer. You know how she suffered. Now the doctors have told my sister that she has less than a year to live. We have always been religious people. How can we believe in God any more?" [1]

Lofton Hudson tells of a wounded soldier whose legs had been amputated. He awakened from surgery to discover that both his legs were gone. He looked at the attendant and said, "It's just like God to do that to me!" [2]

Neither comment or feeling is unusual. Both mentioned God in connection with suffering and pain. The woman seemed surprised; the soldier implied that he expected no better from God; but both mentioned God. George A. Buttrick points out that "For believer and skeptic alike, for faith or unfaith, the fact of pain gets linked with God." [3]

A basic assumption of both the woman and the soldier is that a good God ought to spare us from pain and suffering; however, rather than sparing us, he inflicts pain and suffering on us. On this basis, therefore, many say that there is no God; or if there is, he is not a God of love.

The presence of suffering poses a dilemma for those who believe in a God of love. Here is the way in which the dilemma is often stated: Either God cannot or will not stop the pain and suffering in the world. If he *cannot,* he is not God in the traditional sense of a God with all power. If he *will not,* he is not a God who loves and cares about needy people.

When stated in this way, the dilemma seems hopeless indeed. Archibald MacLeish's drama *J. B.* is a modernized version of Job from a secular point of view. The person playing the role of Satan states the dilemma in this couplet:

> If God is God He is not good;
> If God is good He is not God.[4]

Elton Trueblood points out that the problem of pain should be of intense concern only to a person who assumes that God is good:

> To the one who does not believe that the world is ruled by a Loving Mind, the existence of pain in nature, and the wanton cruelty of man to man, is not the least surprising. There is no reason why he should expect anything else. If there were no God, if reality should be shown to consist of a series of events wholly devoid of meaning and purpose, we might be perplexed, but the presence of evil in the world would be in no way alarming and would demand no special explanation. Even the mild believer need not be deeply concerned. Only when faith is intense and urgent does the problem arise in a really demanding fashion.[5]

Widespread and persistent concern over the problem of evil is impressive evidence for the very thing that the problem seems to deny. Obviously many people still start with faith in a God of love as a basic premise. Even those who vigorously deny such a premise indirectly attest to its persistent and widespread influence. Otherwise, why would professed unbelievers themselves be so concerned with theological implications of pain and injustice?

So it is from the point of view of faith in a God of love that we ask, "Why does God allow so much pain and suffering?"

Pain—Reality or Illusion?

Among the proposed solutions to the dilemma is the suggestion that pain and evil are only illusions. Advocates of this view point out that what seems evil often turns out not to be evil at all. Therefore, they insist that evil and pain are only in the mind: they represent illusions, not reality.

Those who follow the teachings of Christian Science represent the largest group who holds the view that pain is an illusion. Historical Christianity considers this view not only naive but heretical. The Bible clearly teaches that suffering and evil are real. Observation and experience confirm this biblical view.

The average person has difficulty taking seriously the view that evil and pain are unreal. Evil, injustice, pain, and suffering are too rampant to be denied. An unbeliever has said that there is enough suffering in one hospital ward to make atheists of us all. Although believers do not agree with this conclusion, no one can deny the terrible reality and intensity of suffering in a typical hospital ward.

The world is filled with all kinds of pain and suffering. A woman is dying cell by cell and second by second from the slow torture of cancer. A deformed child is born into a lifetime of abnormality and suffering. A husband watches helplessly as his wife's mind and personality wither away into a kind of living death. A father sits helplessly while his daughter fights a hopeless battle with a terminal illness. A child is orphaned and crippled by an automobile accident. A technician's mistake turns a bright, attractive child into little more than a functioning organism. A freak storm robs a man of his house and of his family. An old man is robbed and beaten. A missionary is butchered by fanatics.

When each of these is multiplied by millions, the amount of pain and suffering becomes incomprehensible. Yet this is the kind of world we live in.

The reality of pain and the dilemma it causes becomes most real when the pain becomes personal. The problem of pain is never so acute as when it is *my* pain. This is seen in the biblical account of Job. Job had surely been aware of suffering and pain in the world, but he was never so aware of it until it became his time to sit on the ash heap and scrape his own sores. Then the problem of pain took on a different perspective because it was *his* pain.

C. S. Lewis wrote a book called *The Problem of Pain*. It is a helpful and not unsympathetic treatment of the problem. In the preface Lewis acknowledged his own difficulty in living up to his own principles.[6] Years later he wrote another book about pain—a much more personal book. His wife was dying of cancer, and he chronicled his doubts and questions as he suffered with her through her agony. *A Grief Observed* [7] reads like the book of Job. The reasons for the similarity are that both Job and C. S. Lewis were men of faith and were trying to cope with pain as a personal experience, not as a matter of philosophical inquiry.

Suffering and Sin

Thornton Wilder in his novel *The Bridge of San Luis Rey* [8] probes the question of why tragedies happen. He tells of an accident. An ancient bridge gives way, and five persons fall to their death into the chasm below. In the background are deep questions: Why did the accident happen just when it did? Why was each of these people involved? Was it all by chance, or was there some purpose in it?

The earliest strata of biblical revelation reflected a time when the problem of pain was solved by saying that suffering and pain were punishment by God against sinners. The book of Job challenged this traditional view. The book destroyed the old idea that all suffering is the result of sin.

Many people have never appreciated this insight. They have not moved beyond the position held by Job's three friends. They still think of suffering as punishment for sin. When trouble befalls others, they assume that the sufferers are being punished for sins.

When trouble comes to themselves, their first response usually is "What have I done to deserve this?"

The highest strata of biblical revelation helps to clarify the relation between suffering and sin:

1. *Human sin is a general factor in explaining the presence of pain and suffering in the world.*—Paul seemed to assume this in Romans 8:20-22. Just as humanity needs redemption, so does the created order. The creation itself has been marked and flawed by sin. Paul may have had in mind the Genesis account of the immediate consequences of Adam and Eve's sin. The pleasant environment of the garden of Eden was replaced by a world in which struggle, pain, and toil are realities (Gen. 3:14-19).

2. *Sin is sometimes a causal factor in personal pain and suffering.*—The law of sin and retribution is a reality, and the retribution does sometimes take the form of evils we inflict on ourselves by our own actions. Also, our sinful choices and habits do hurt and blight others. Paul described God's wrath at work by allowing people to make their own choices and to reap the inevitable consequences of their sins (Rom. 1:18-32; notice the words "God gave them up" in vv. 24,26,28).

3. *There is not always a direct causal relation between suffering and sin.*—The book of Job utterly demolishes the view that suffering is always punishment for sin. Job's three friends insisted that Job's sufferings had to be due to sins he had committed. Job did not claim to be perfect; however, he knew that he had committed no sin that deserved such disasters as had befallen him. At the end of the book the Lord vindicated Job and rebuked Job's friends.

The same issue arose when Jesus and his disciples encountered the man born blind. They asked, "Rabbi, who sinned, this man or his parents, that he was born blind?" (John 9:2). Jesus told them that their basic assumption was wrong. The man's plight was not due to sin—either his or his parents.

4. *Suffering can always be the occasion for a person to draw near to God.* —The early Christian community prayed when one of its members was faced with suffering and sickness. Part of this praying involved the mutual confession of sins—by the praying community and by the praying sufferer (Jas. 5:13–16).

Luke 13:1–5 records a significant episode in Jesus' ministry. Some people reported two disasters to Jesus. One disaster was the execution of some Galileans by Pilate; the other was the death of eighteen persons caused by the collapse of a tower. Apparently some people were assuming that these disasters proved the sinfulness of the persons killed. Jesus refused to allow such a smug attitude. He pointed out that the only moral lesson anyone should draw from such disasters is a personal one—our own need for repentance. If the disaster highlights anyone's sins, it highlights the sins of those who stand aside and pass judgment on the victims.

In Wilder's novel a priest saw the collapse of the bridge and the death of the five victims. The priest shared the false assumption of Job's three friends. Therefore, he set out to explain the disaster as an act of God's justice. He did painstaking research into the lives of the five victims; however, the evidence did not enable him to prove his thesis. There may have been a pattern there, but he was unable to find it.

The Mystery of God's Will

Hand in hand with the view that suffering is always the result of sin goes the idea that God is directly responsible for everything that happens. The early Hebrews ignored secondary causes and attributed all things directly to God. The book of Job challenged the traditional explanation for suffering at two points. It challenged the view that all suffering is punishment for sin. It also challenged the view that God is directly responsible for human suffering. God is presented as allowing but not as inflicting Job's suffering.

Many people still think of God as directly responsible for everything that happens. Every disaster is attributed to the all-encompassing term "the will of God." Leslie Weatherhead wrote a book called *The Will of God*. He warned against the dangers of blaming everything on "the will of God." For example, a person may refer to both a tragic accident and the quiet death of an aged saint as the will of God. Weatherhead suggested that we distinguish between what God wants (his intentional will), what he allows (his circumstantial will), and what he finally brings to pass (his ultimate will). He acknowledged that all things, of course, are *within* the will of God in an all-inclusive sense; but he felt that we must distinguish what God wants from what he allows.[9]

Recognizing this fact by no means solves the problem of pain, but it does alleviate it somewhat. If we attribute everything directly to God, we make it very difficult to defend the goodness of God. How can he be good and loving if he inflicts so much suffering?

However, we must ask: Have we sacrificed God's power by seeking to protect his goodness? If God is not directly in responsible control of all things, how can we speak of him as *almighty* God?

C. S. Lewis refused to get hung on this horn of the dilemma. He maintained that the dilemma itself is open to considerable misunderstanding—especially the words *good* and *almighty* as they are popularly used with reference to God. Lewis said that this is the way in which the dilemma is usually stated: "If God were good, He would wish to make His creatures perfectly happy, and if God were almighty, He would be able to do what He wished. But the creatures are not happy. Therefore God lacks utter goodness, or power, or both." [10] Lewis pointed out that the problem with this statement of the dilemma is the popular meaning of the words *good* and *almighty*. The dilemma is unanswerable if the popular meanings are assumed; therefore, we need to probe the meaning of both words.

How Can We Believe in a God of Love When There Is So Much Suffering? 37

Lewis began by probing the word *almighty*. He faced the crucial question head-on. When we say that God is almighty or omnipotent, do we mean that God can do anything? The facts of our own experience plus the insights of the Bible lead us to recognize that God has chosen to limit his own power in certain ways.

For example, when God made man free, he thereby imposed a certain limit on what he would do in dealing with humanity. Freedom is one of our greatest blessings, but it is also beset with great peril. God allows men to make their own choices, but he also allows us to reap the harvest of our own choices. As we have already seen, this is the clue to the moral evil in the world and the explanation for much of the pain and suffering that results from human sin—either the suffering a person inflicts on himself or the pain he inflicts on others. When God made us free, this kind of pain became a very real possibility.

There is also a sense in which God has given a certain freedom to the universe itself. This is an area of great mystery, for it relates to the natural evil that befalls us—pain for which there is no discernible reason—pain that is not caused (at least directly) by human sin. No one has any final answers or easy solutions in this area.

All of us can recognize that much suffering flows from the operation of certain processes in nature. Water is essential for life. It slacks our thirst, but a person also can drown in water. Likewise, fire can warm us and cook our food; yet it also can burn us and cause great pain.

Part of the way in which God has limited himself is in placing us in a universe in which certain orderly processes are at work. This does not mean that ours is a universe that runs by ironclad, unchangeable rules. God is no celestial Clockmaker who has made the universe, wound it up, and now has left it to tick away according to its own mechanism. This is God's universe; he knows and cares; he sometimes moves in ways that seem miraculous by those who assume that natural laws are fixed and rigid. On the other hand, God is not constantly intervening to change certain ordered processes of nature. (See chap. 5 for more on this point.)

Good Out of Evil

When we say that God allows evil but does not inflict it, we have alleviated the problem somewhat. However, the problem is still far from solved. The question still remains, *why* does he allow it? One possible answer has been hinted at: He allows it because of the benefits that come from human freedom and an ordered universe. In other words, he allows pain because of the good that can come from allowing the circumstances out of which pain sometimes comes. A similar but further answer also sometimes is given: God allows pain and suffering because good can come out of pain and suffering.

Just as C. S. Lewis boldly challenged the popular definition of divine omnipotence, so did he challenge the popular definition of divine goodness. Lewis pointed out that we tend to attribute to God a sentimental kind of goodness: "The problem of reconciling human suffering with the existence of a God who loves, is insoluble so long as we attach a trivial meaning to the word 'love,' and look on things as if man were the centre of them. Man is not the centre. God does not exist for the sake of man. Man does not exist for his own sake." [11]

Is God's highest purpose for humanity that we live a pain-free existence? Does he not have some nobler and more positive purpose in mind? Do pain and suffering not sometimes contribute to the achieving of God's good purpose for us?

Romans 8:28 is the most memorable biblical statement on the theme of God's good purpose: "We know that in everything God works for good with those who love him, who are called according to his purpose." In the next verse God's good purpose is described as conformity to the image of his Son.

The great value of this verse is not that it explains suffering but that it affirms God's good purpose. Paul did not say that God is directly responsible for all things; what he said was that "in everything God works for good."

Paul did not try to explain specific instances of human suffering. However, he did affirm that God is at work in everything—including pain and suffering—to work out his good purpose for us. For example, Paul spent several years as a prisoner. This must have been a trying experience for a world traveler like Paul. Yet Paul found ways in which this trial could serve a good purpose. Thus he wrote from prison to the Philippians that his imprisonment had been the occasion for many guards to hear the gospel and for other believers to be emboldened by the apostle's example (Phil. 1:12–14).

This testimony has been echoed by innumerable saints down through the centuries. No normal person volunteers for the school of suffering. Suffering and pain are always bad experiences. And yet, often we learn some of life's most important lessons in the school of suffering.

T. B. Maston wrote *Suffering—a Personal Perspective*. He said:

> Our older son, Tom Mc, was injured at birth. He has spent his life, more than forty years now, in a wheelchair. He is far more seriously handicapped than most cerebral palsied. Every voluntary muscle in his body is affected. He cannot talk, walk, or sit alone. His mother or daddy has to do everything for him.[12]

Looking back, this concerned father bears this testimony of trust in a heavenly Father:

> The presence of a handicapped child in the house, as well as suffering in general, can and will be used of God to deepen and enrich our lives if we react rightly to it. We are sure that our Heavenly Father has used our own experience to enable us to be more sympathetic with people who suffer and more helpful in our relations with them. We believe also that Tom Mc has been a real blessing, in a personal way, to many who have come to know

him. In other words, our testimony is that life, in some way, compensates for whatever suffering overtakes us, if we will react properly to it.[13]

Trusting When We Cannot Explain

As we have noted, this is one of countless testimonies from persons who have found some good emerge from painful circumstances. However, neither this fact nor any other point made thus far offers a satisfying rational answer to the question "Why does God allow so much pain and suffering?" "That *some* evil is the condition of the highest good seems clear, but why should there be so much of it?" [14]

Is there then no satisfying rational answer to the question? This is the same kind of question we faced in chapter 1. If a person is looking for scientific or rational proof of God's existence, he will be disappointed. There is evidence, but there is not proof—at least not the kind many people seek. The same is true of explaining why God allows so much pain. There are clues that suggest the possibility of explaining some things, but there is no thoroughgoing explanation for it all. Yet we are not left without evidence of our basic premise—that God is good. Again we do not have proof, but we do have evidence—the evidence of history and of personal experience. To some, the evidence of much pain and suffering seems to outweigh the evidence for a God of love. Believers also are aware of pain and suffering. They feel it. They shrink from it. They seek relief from it. They struggle with it. Yet even as they do, they still trust that God is good.

Why do we persist in this trust? "The Christian clings to his faith, not because he allows nothing to count against it, but because he believes that his evidence for believing in God's love is more compelling than the evidence that counts against it." [15] First of all, we trust God because of the nature of Christianity. The heart of our faith is the cross and resurrection. George A. Buttrick made

How Can We Believe in a God of Love When There Is So Much Suffering?   41

a thorough study of the entire subject of *God, Pain, and Evil*. He concludes that although there is no rational explanation for suffering, there is a redemptive event that helps us. That event is the resurrection: "The light of the Resurrection means that God is in the Cross. He is with us in all our pains in both love and power." [16]

The cross clearly shows us that God is not an impassive observer of the human scene. Rather, he is actively involved to the ultimate degree. In the cross God suffered with us and for us.

The resurrection declares the good news that God will never let pain and death have the last word. Beyond suffering and death are life and resurrection.

Thus Christians respond to pain and suffering with faith and hope because of God's revelation and redemption in the death and resurrection of Jesus Christ.

A second reason why Christians trust God's goodness is their own experience of God's goodness. Believers see every good experience as from the hand of a loving Father (Jas. 1:17). And as we have seen, they even dare to see the hand of God bringing good out of life's hurts (Rom. 8:28).

And a third reason is this: Trust is a better choice than its alternative. I cannot prove to a convinced unbeliever that God is good. However, as already stated in chapter 1, believing in a God who cares is just as plausible and much more satisfying than believing that the universe is a cosmic accident. I had far rather face life's joys and sorrows with trust in a God who suffers with us and for us and who says that the final word is not *pain* or *death* but *life*!

Reading John Claypool's book *Tracks of a Fellow Struggler* is a heartrending yet helpful experience. We walk with this father-pastor through the shock of learning that his daughter had leukemia and through the pain of watching her suffer, then losing her to death. Claypool tells how he tried to find a way to respond to his loss. He tried what he calls "the road of unquestioning resignation." He also tried "the road of total intellectual understanding." He found that the first road was neither honest nor an expression of real faith in a God who cares. He found that the second road provided no satisfying answers. He found a third road to be the best. He calls this "the road of gratitude." This road does not accept pain without struggles, questions, even doubts; on the other hand, neither does it demand satisfying answers to all questions, especially the ultimate question *Why*. This is the road of gratitude and trust.[17]

C. S. Lewis watched his beloved wife die of cancer. He recorded in notebooks his feelings at various stages in this ordeal. These notebooks later were published as *A Grief Observed*. The book reads remarkably like the book of Job. The careful logic of his earlier book *The Problem of Pain* is replaced by the anguished questions of a sufferer. Lewis found that he had far more questions than he could find answers for.

"When I lay these questions before God I get no answer. But a rather special sort of 'No answer.' It is not the locked door. It is more like a silent, certainly not uncompassionate, gaze. As though He shook His head not in refusal but waiving the question. Like, 'Peace, child; you don't understand.' " [18]

In the end Lewis settled for such a situation because he dared to trust God. He discovered anew that God's ways remain a mystery to us just as life itself is a mystery. We cannot deny the mystery; neither can we solve it. If we choose to do so, we can shake our fists at the One beyond the mystery—or we can dare to trust him.

Lewis' last paragraph was written after his wife's death. His poignant words testify both to his faith and hers: "How wicked it would be, if we could, to call the dead back! She said not to me but to the chaplain, 'I am at peace with God.' She smiled, but not at me." [19]

3
How Can We Believe What the New Testament Says About Jesus?

On January 14, 1968 Malcolm Muggeridge dropped a bombshell on the intellectual world of our day. The occasion was an address at the University of Edinburgh. The bombshell was Muggeridge's announcement of Christian faith. He described his disillusionment with proposed solutions to the ills of society. Then he said:

> So I come back to where I began, to that other king, one Jesus; to the Christian notion that man's efforts to make himself personally and collectively happy in earthly terms are doomed to failure. He must indeed, as Christ said, be born again, be a new man, or he's nothing. So at least I have concluded, having failed to find in past experience, present dilemmas, and future expectations any alternative proposition. As far as I am concerned, it is Christ or nothing.[1]

People in the United States are not as familiar with Muggeridge as the people of Great Britain. Britons know him as the one-time editor of *Punch,* a skilled journalist, a witty satirist, a television personality. Many Britons were shocked by Muggeridge's announcement. In Great Britain, even more than in the United States, Christianity is generally not even considered as a possible solution for human needs or as a personal choice for an intelligent person.

If Muggeridge had professed faith in secular humanism, no one would have batted an eye. Secular humanism—the belief that mankind can build a brave new world without God—is the faith of many intellectuals. If Muggeridge had sounded a note of cynical despair, few would have considered this newsworthy. After all, satirists are usually cynics. If Muggeridge had announced that he was dabbling in religion—something like Transcendental Meditation—this probably would not have attracted much attention. Such religious fads are the stock-in-trade of some people—even intellectuals. If Muggeridge had made a mildly "Christian" statement, even this probably would have created little stir. Talk of Jesus as a good man and great teacher is not completely unacceptable in proper academic circles.

However, Muggeridge horrified his peers by announcing his commitment to Christ in much stronger words. Since then, Muggeridge has had many opportunities to explain his faith. His book *Jesus Rediscovered* is a collection of some of his writings, speeches, and interviews. He explained the intellectual basis for his commitment to Christ. He had become more and more disenchanted with proposed materialistic solutions to man's needs. While seeking a viable alternative, his attention was increasingly drawn to the ancient claims of the Christian faith. Finally he concluded that Christ is far better than any alternative.[2]

The reaction to Muggeridge's conversion underscores the need for this chapter. The unique claims of Christian faith continue to be a scandal to nearly everyone—not only to the atheists but also to those who believe in God but not in the deity of Jesus Christ. They ask, "How can we believe what the New Testament says about Jesus Christ?"

God Was in Christ

First of all, we need to clarify what the New Testament teaches about Jesus Christ. One of the most beautiful benedictions in the Bible is 2 Corinthians 13:14: "The grace of the Lord Jesus Christ

How Can We Believe What the New Testament Says About Jesus?

and the love of God and the fellowship of the Holy Spirit be with you all." Notice that Paul began with "the grace of the Lord Jesus Christ." This points to the daring and uniquely Christian claim about Jesus Christ: God has chosen to make himself known in Jesus Christ; therefore, Jesus is the focal point for our knowledge of God.

In chapter 1 we traced three kinds of evidence that point toward belief in God: the created universe that bears marks of the Creator, the moral and religious experiences of human beings, and the events of biblical history that point to God's action. In that chapter we were interested primarily in the question "How can we believe in God?" rather than in the question "What kind of God can we believe in?"

Theologians speak of general revelation and of special revelation. General revelation is the revelation of God in nature. Special revelation is the revelation of God in the events recorded in the Bible, especially in Jesus Christ. If we had only God's revelation in nature, we at best could see evidences of an intelligent and powerful force behind the universe. However, the most basic questions would remain unanswered: Is this force personal or impersonal? If personal, is God friendly or unfriendly?

Many people in our country would quickly say that God is personal and loving. But what is their basis for this belief? The basis for faith in a loving heavenly Father is Jesus Christ. His teachings, his life, his death, his resurrection—they all testify to the God of grace and love.

Sometimes a person will say, "I believe that Jesus is God's Son because he is so like God." This, however, is the reverse of the Christian position, which says, "I believe that God is a loving Father because I see him in Jesus Christ." Leonard Griffith states the issue clearly:

> We try to settle our doubts by deciding whether Jesus is really like God. If we were honest we should reverse the order and

realize that all we know about God with any certainty we have learned from Jesus. Christianity does not look from God to Jesus; rather it looks from Jesus to God; and it is a real question whether, apart from Jesus, we should be able to form any clear picture of God at all.[3]

In other words, the New Testament does not say that Jesus is like God but that God is like Jesus. And, as D. M. Baillie has pointed out, a true statement of faith in Christ "will tell us not simply that God is *like* Christ, but that God was *in* Christ." [4]

Jesus was not just a good man who helped people and taught them to trust in a heavenly Father. The New Testament presents God in Christ revealing himself by acting on behalf of sinful, needy humanity. When Jesus was asked by Philip, "Lord, show us the Father, and we shall be satisfied," Jesus replied: "Have I been with you so long, and yet you do not know me, Philip? He who has seen me has seen the Father" (John 14:8–9).

Is Christ the Only Way?

Such claims scandalize many people. They can accept Jesus as a prophet, as a good man, and as a great teacher; however, they cannot bring themselves to accept him as the Son of God through whom God has made himself known in a unique way. They ask: "What about other religions? What about believing in God but not believing in Jesus as God's Son?"

The scope of this book does not include room for a lengthy discussion of comparative religions. However, enough needs to be said to speak to the central issue involved. First of all, it should be said that the Christian claim is that Jesus Christ is the primary channel but not the only channel of divine revelation. The primary focus of divine revelation was through the line of Abraham, Isaac, and Jacob in Old Testament times and then supremely in Jesus Christ. However, while God worked most intensely to bring his revelation and redemption into sharp focus in the events recorded in the Bible, he also operated on the stage of world history. He worked more generally, but he worked. Thus there are elements of truth in most of the world's great religions. However, the truth is much less clearly focused than in Christ; and in many cases it is mixed with a good deal of superstition and error about God, humanity, and the world.

The picture of God as a loving, caring Father is most sharply drawn in Christianity. Some pagan religions present a completely different view of God. Others have traces of an idea of God's grace, but nothing as sharp and clear as embodiment of God in Christ.

Christ and his way stand in contrast to other religions at another basic point—not only in revelation but also in redemption. Generally speaking, other religions assume that man is the active person in making himself acceptable to God or the gods. Man—either by his goodness, his piety, his mysticism, or his ritual—is able to become acceptable to God or to put himself in harmony with spiritual reality. By contrast, Christ represents a way of God's grace reaching down to sinful humanity. God by his grace saves us and makes us his own children. Thus the basic movement is from God to humanity, not vice versa.

This contrast holds even when Christianity and Judaism are compared. Insofar as the Old Testament is seen as a revelation of a God of grace, it foreshadows the supreme act of God's grace in Christ. Christianity has its roots deep in the Old Testament, which itself testifies to the need for something more. Jeremiah, for example, acknowledged the limitations of the old covenant and foretold a new covenant based on direct access to God through his grace (Jer. 31:31–34). Christians believe that this new covenant was established by God in and through Jesus Christ. Jesus Christ is the Mediator, but not in the sense of a go-between; rather, God comes to us and offers himself to us in Jesus Christ.

And what about the many people of no particular religious persuasion who believe in God but not in Christ? Many of these people even profess to believe in the God of love about whom Jesus taught, but they cannot bring themselves to believe in Jesus as Son of God. They believe that Jesus was a good man and a wise teacher, but not the Son of God.

The fallacy in this is that we cannot separate Jesus' teaching about God from Jesus' claims to embody God's love in himself. On what basis can we believe what Jesus taught about God's love and yet reject the crucial element in all of Jesus' teachings? If Jesus was not right about being the embodiment of God and his love, why should we believe his teachings about God as a heavenly Father? If Jesus was not God's Son, why did he claim to be? Was he deliberately lying? Or was he himself deluded and confused? In either case, how can we trust anything he said and did? Of course, the other possibility is that Jesus was right—about himself and about God's love.

If Jesus was a good man and a wise teacher, he also was the Son of God as he claimed. If he was not the Son of God, he was neither a good man nor a wise teacher. C. S. Lewis stated in the strongest possible terms the choice we have: "A man who was merely a man and said the sort of things Jesus said would not be a great moral teacher. He would either be a lunatic . . . or else he would be the Devil of Hell. You must make your choice. Either this man was, and is, the Son of God: or else a madman or something worse." [5]

Can We Trust the New Testament?

Of course, there is another possibility: The New Testament could be wrong in what it tells us about Jesus Christ. Many people opt for this explanation of the facts. Few doubt the historical phenomenon of Jesus of Nazareth, but some question the New Testament's record and explanation of this phenomenon. According to these critics, Jesus was only a great and good man—a teacher of love toward God and others. Jesus never claimed to be any more than this; however, Jesus' zealous followers later made him into a

Godlike figure. They even went so far as to put words into his mouth that he never spoke. In other words, the New Testament does not accurately represent what Jesus said and did but what the church later wrote that he said and did.

As you can see, this is a serious charge. Christianity has its roots in a historical revelation; and if that history is inaccurate, then the entire revelation is changed and undercut. William Hordern makes this point in a striking way:

> The importance of the picture of Jesus that is given in the Gospels can be shown by a crude illustration. Suppose that, historically, it became evident that Jesus did not bless little children, but kicked them out of his way; he did not forgive his enemies, but cursed them; he did not chase the money changers out of the Temple, but expropriated one of their tables to make money for himself. In that case, Christian faith would be radically different. If God became man in this child-kicking, enemy-cursing, money changer, we would have to confess that God is radically different from what Christians have proclaimed him to be. If we accept the Christian faith that Jesus Christ is the incarnation of God, then we must take seriously the historical nature of the person of Jesus.[6]

But how can we be sure that the New Testament record is trustworthy and accurate? The New Testament books, especially the Gospels, are the primary sources for the Christian faith. How can we be sure that the writers did not distort and misinterpret what happened—either intentionally or unintentionally?

Most New Testament scholars point out that there was at least a generation between Jesus' resurrection and the writing down of the Gospels. During those years the life and teachings about Jesus were told and retold by word of mouth. It was during this period that some critics claim the church distorted the true facts about Jesus and his teachings.

How reasonable is it to assume intentional distortion? Consider the kind of people who wrote the New Testament. They were people who strongly believed in truth and integrity—so much so that many of them were willing to die for what they believed. Would such people deliberately distort the truth? Would they build a system of truth on a deliberate lie? Would they then die for it? The writers of the New Testament obviously did select some material from Jesus' life and teachings that spoke most clearly to their needs a generation after Jesus' resurrection. But this does not mean that they distorted it to fit their needs. William Hordern notes a parallel from American history: "Lincoln's Gettysburg Address obviously has been remembered because it speaks to certain needs of the American people, but by no logic does it follow that it was invented by later Americans to meet those needs." [7]

What about the charge that the New Testament writers unintentionally distorted the truth? Keep in mind that the verbal and written reports were under the direction and constant scrutiny of many eyewitnesses. Not all the New Testament writers were eyewitnesses, but they reported what eyewitnesses had told and retold. Any distortions of the gospel story would have been quickly corrected under the direction of those who had been with Jesus.

The Declaration of Independence is the key document of the American Revolution. Suppose someone charged that the document is not historically accurate. Instead, so the imaginary charge goes, it was written after the war in an attempt to portray our forebears as men of courageous commitment to human freedom. Among the strongest arguments against such a theory would be these: (1) The Declaration of Independence fits the events of 1776 as known from other sources: it is the most credible explanation for the severing of political bonds with Great Britain. (2) What we know of the early leaders of our nation makes it difficult to believe that they would found the nation on a lie. (3) What we know of American history since 1776 is consistent with the commitment to human freedom stated in the Declaration of Independence.

A similar situation exists with reference to the New Testament:

(1) The New Testament fits what happened in the first century; it gives the most credible explanation for the origin of the Christian religion. (2) What we know of the early leaders makes it difficult to believe they would found the way of truth on a lie. (3) There is consistency at many points between the origins of the Christian faith as set forth in the New Testament and the subsequent impact of Christianity. The events recorded in the Gospels literally divided history.

Are Miracles Possible?

But someone may say: "The Gospels do not record the same kind of history as do the records of the American Revolution. The Gospels tell of miraculous events, and everyone knows that miracles do not happen."

Thus the prejudice against miracles lies at the heart of much skepticism about the New Testament and about Jesus himself. This prejudice explains why many people can speak respectfully of a purely human Jesus but cannot bring themselves even to consider the supernatural Jesus who is reported in the Gospels.

As we have already noted, the Gospels present Jesus as claiming to be the Son of God. The entire framework of Jesus' life is miraculous. The nature of his coming was a miracle. During his life on earth he performed miracles. His resurrection was the greatest miracle of all. The whole idea of the incarnation—God in flesh—is unapologetically miraculous.

If we take the New Testament seriously, we are forced to reckon with its claims about miracles. Alan Richardson points out: "If our judgment were to be decided by strictly historical considerations and by nothing else, we could not avoid the conclusion that Jesus worked miracles. The evidence that Jesus worked miracles is just as strong, and is of precisely the same quality and texture, as that He taught that God is Father and that His disciples should forgive one another." [8]

However, miracles are ruled out not on the basis of an objective examination of the historical evidence but on the basis of a presupposition that begins by ruling out the possibility of miracles. A naturalistic presupposition by definition rules out any possibility of the supernatural. In the name of being scientific and objective, naturalists rule out miracles by assuming that "the only forces in the universe are those which physical science can measure and describe, but that is a philosophical and not a scientific assumption." [9]

The eighteenth-century philosopher David Hume presented the classic exposition of the naturalistic view. Hume began with the assumption that nature is a closed system operating under completely uniform laws. This assumption, then, rules out any possibility of miracles. Hume wrote: "A miracle is a violation of the laws of nature; and as a firm and unalterable experience has established these laws, the proof against a miracle, from the very nature of the fact, is as entire as any argument from experience can possibly be imagined." [10] Hume therefore concluded, in effect, that any report of a miracle must be either a lie or a mistake.

How objective is an approach that rules out all reports of miracles as lies or mistakes? The reports cannot be judged by their own merits because they are prejudged to be reports of what could not have happened. C. S. Lewis accused Hume of evading the real question:

> The question, "Do miracles occur?" and the question, "Is the course of Nature uniform?" are the same question asked in two different ways. Hume, by sleight of hand, treats them as two different questions. He first answers, "Yes," to the question whether Nature is absolutely uniform: and then uses this "Yes" as a ground for answering, "No," to the question, "Do miracles occur?" The single real question which he set out to answer is never discussed at all.[11]

Lewis conceded that there is strong basis for assuming a general uniformity in nature, but he insisted that only the purest naturalism can insist on *absolute* uniformity. To be consistent the naturalist must assume that "nothing can come into Nature from the outside because there is nothing outside to come in, Nature being everything." [12] Nothing other than purely naturalistic explanations can be accepted for anything. If a person admits some force in the universe beyond this natural order, he has at least opened the door to the possibility of miracle. If a person admits the possibility of any intrusion from beyond nature, the whole fabric of naturalism collapses. It stands as a total closed system, or it does not stand at all.

This is especially true if one admits the possibility of God. Admit God and you have admitted the possibility of miracles. The Deists, of course, claimed that God had created the natural laws and then let the universe operate by these laws with no interference from him. There is considerable truth in this. God did create essentially an orderly universe. However, what evidence do we have that God does not operate within and through his creation? Christians believe that ours is an orderly universe and that this condition is a great blessing. Since God made the universe, God also can operate within it as he chooses. The Bible does not present God as constantly and capriciously intervening in the orderly processes of his creation. However, the Bible affirms not only that God is at work within the orderly processes of his universe but also that God has revealed himself through actions that seem to break into the usual order of things.

Physical science neither proves nor disproves miracles. However, modern scientific models tend to undercut the rigid and closed naturalism of earlier generations. Science seeks and still finds basic patterns of order. Eric Rust points out that this is true not only of the life sciences but also of such bastions of naturalism as physics: "The mechanistic model with its ideas of rigid determinism has disappeared . . . from contemporary physics." He explains: "Determinism has been replaced by indeterminancy, and physical laws become descriptions of the expected behavior of an assembly of particles, that is to say, they are statistical. That such statistical averages would normally be expected is a far cry from the model of a machinelike universe whose laws could never be broken." [13] This, of course, does not prove miracles, but it does show the fallacy of denying their possibility on the basis of a machinelike view of the universe.

Augustine pointed out that miracles are not contrary to nature, but to what is known about nature. Thus it is misleading to define miracles as intrusions into the natural order of things. Our knowledge of the "natural order of things" is much more limited than that of him who created all things and works in and through them to bring about his will. The best definition of miracle is that sense of awesome awareness that God was or is at work in an event to bring about his will. This definition takes into account those "miraculous" phenomena that man's knowledge may sometimes better explain and those phenomena that may forever defy any human explanation.[14]

The Bible affirms divine Providence at work throughout human history and experiences. Yet it strongly declares that the central focus of God's revelation and redemption took place in certain key events. Although miracle is inherent in the entire scope of biblical history, there is a much more judicious presentation of miracles than is generally recognized. Actually, most of the biblical miracles are reported in connection with three great critical times in redemptive history: the Exodus, the Baal crisis (when paganism threatened to overwhelm the faith of Israel), and in the events related to Jesus Christ. From the Christian perspective the heart of divine revelation and redemption is recorded in the Gospels. They tell of God's unique actions in the coming, life, ministry, death, and resurrection of Jesus Christ.

C. S. Lewis offered a principle by which to judge the intrinsic probability of a reported miracle. Judge it by "the innate fitness of things." Lewis pointed out that the miracles of the Gospels rate high in probability when judged by the criterion of our sense of fitness to life and history. He suggested the following analogy:

> Let us suppose we possess parts of a novel or a symphony. Someone now brings us a newly discovered piece of manuscript and says, "This is the missing part of the work. This is the chapter on which the whole plot of the novel really turned. This is the main theme of the symphony." Our business would be to see whether the new passage, if admitted to the central place which the discoverer claimed for it, did actually illumine all the parts we had already seen and "pull them together." [15]

The Gospel account of the incarnate Savior is the key chapter of human history, the main theme of the symphony of human life. Apart from Christ history seems like an endless series of cycles going nowhere. Christ is the midpoint of human history from which history takes its meaning. It has come from somewhere, and it is going somewhere. And the clue to past, present, and future is Jesus Christ.

Many theories have been proposed to try to explain the phenomenon of Jesus Christ. The most plausible and certainly the most satisfying explanation remains the explanation given in the Gospels. This point is nowhere so clearly demonstrated as when we examine various explanations for the miracle of resurrection.

What About the Resurrection?

David Hume ruled out the resurrection of Jesus on the basis that no dead person comes back to life. The evidence is ignored; it is not even examined. It is ruled out on the assumption that resurrection is impossible. As we have seen, this is hardly an objective approach. Christians are aware that dead men do not come back to life; however, they are convinced that Jesus did. They recognize that this is a miracle—the ultimate miracle, but they believe it because the evidence is so strong.

Historians claim that they cannot verify the resurrection of Jesus by historical data. However, they can verify the historical fact of the resurrection faith. Clearly the early Christians *believed* that Jesus had been raised from the dead. The historical evidence for this fact is beyond question. The real question is, "How do we explain the existence of this faith?"

Something happened that sent the followers out into the ancient world as flaming evangels. People referred to them as those who "turned the world upside down" (Acts 17:6). The Christians themselves acted as they did because they believed that Jesus was alive—that he had conquered death and that he had commissioned them as his witnesses. The question is, "What is the most plausible explanation for this phenomenon?"

The New Testament explanation, of course, is that they believed it because Jesus was indeed raised from the dead. In spite of Jesus' repeated predictions that he would be crucified and raised from the dead, his followers were surprised by both events. After his death they had no expectation of his resurrection. When they first heard that the tomb was empty, they concluded only that someone had moved the body. When the first reports of his resurrection were shared, the disciples refused to believe the reports. In fact, Luke 24:11 says that the first reports seemed to the apostles to comprise nothing but "an idle tale."

Thus Thomas was not the only doubter; they all were doubters. They were not expecting the resurrection; and they believed only when they were absolutely convinced by seeing the risen Lord. "The disciples were not believing. They had lost hope. Something had to happen to create their faith. It was not faith which created the experience of the appearances, but the appearances which created belief in the resurrection." [16]

This is one explanation for the phenomenon of the resurrection faith. What other explanations are possible? Over the years a

How Can We Believe What the New Testament Says About Jesus?

number of theories have been proposed in an attempt to explain the resurrection faith in some way other than the way it is explained in the New Testament.

One of the theories is the hoax theory. According to this view, the disciples took the body of Jesus; then they spread the lie that they had seen him alive. Matthew 28:11–15 reports how the guards at the tomb were bribed to say that Jesus' disciples had stolen Jesus' body while they slept.

If this theory is true, the apostles pulled off the most colossal hoax of all times. Let us assume for a moment that this is actually what happened. How then can one explain the later actions of the apostles? They went forth to turn the ancient world upside down. They boldly proclaimed their risen Lord, and they suffered and died for him. The inescapable question is this: Would they have given their lives for a hoax?

Another theory, sometimes called the swoon theory, is that Jesus never died on the cross. The disciples thought he was dead, so they placed his body in the tomb. However, Jesus revived and left the tomb. Therefore the disciples did see Jesus after his "death," but he had never actually been dead.

This theory raises a number of questions: How could everyone—including the Roman soldiers—be wrong about Jesus' death? What later happened to Jesus? What kind of person would allow his followers to build their faith on what Jesus knew to be a lie?

Hugh J. Schonfield attempts to answer the first of these questions. In his book *The Passover Plot*, he offers his own reconstruction of what happened. He assumes that Jesus plotted with Joseph of Arimathea and other unnamed conspirators (but not any of the apostles). The plot called for Jesus to receive a drug that would make him appear to be dead. Then after Joseph helped him get out of the tomb, Jesus would appear to his followers as one risen from the dead. According to Schonfield, the sponge filled with vinegar

(Mark 15:36) contained the drug. However, the plot failed. The soldier's spear mortally wounded Jesus. He lived long enough to talk with Joseph, but he died in the tomb on Saturday.

Any form of this theory is much more incredible than the New Testament account of the resurrection miracle. The theory also raises a serious moral problem. Would Jesus have plotted to deceive his own followers and to build his kingdom on a lie? Schonfield tries to exonerate Jesus by claiming that he acted in what he thought to be the best interests of all concerned. However, it is hard to believe that the Jesus of the Gospels would have schemed to deceive, even for the best of motives.

The mistaken identity theory assumes that the disciples did see something or someone whom they mistook for Jesus. This is Schonfield's tentative explanation for how the disciples came to believe Jesus was alive. Schonfield hypothesizes an unknown young man who was very loyal to Jesus. He was the one who gave him the drug. He also was with Jesus in the tomb. Jesus told him to go and tell Peter and the others that the Messiah had been raised according to the Scriptures. This young man was later seen by Mary Magdalene, who mistook him for Jesus. The other appearances also were encounters with this man. Schonfield is not dogmatic at this point, but this is as close as he comes to offering an explanation for the resurrection faith of the early Christians.

But how could this man have deceived not only Mary but all the others who saw him? Schonfield makes this admission:

> Naturally it cannot be said that this is the solution of the puzzle. The men may not have been in every case the same. There is room for other theories, such as that the man concerned, if there was but one, was a medium, and that Jesus, risen from the dead into the After Life in the Spiritualist sense, spoke through him in his own voice, which enabled his presence to be recognised. Too little is told, and that little quickly became too legendary, and too contradictory, for any assured conclusion.[17]

Schonfield seems to have come to his theory because of two basic presuppositions: (1) Jesus could not have been raised from the dead. (2) The New Testament does not present an accurate, credible account of what really happened. Schonfield assumes that someone (himself in this case), twenty centuries removed from the fact, can take the "confused" testimonies of eyewitnesses and discover what really happened. Believing this calls for more "blind" faith than accepting the obvious miracle described in the Gospels. Imagine rejecting the miracle of resurrection and proposing instead that Jesus' spirit spoke to his followers through a medium! Amazing indeed are the lengths to which a convinced unbeliever will go to avoid accepting the Bible's explanation for what happened!

Faith Is Commitment

This chapter has focused on the question "Why should we believe what the New Testament says about Jesus?" One answer is that Jesus Christ as God's Son embodies the highest revelation of a God of mercy and grace. Another answer is that the New Testament record of Jesus' life, death, and resurrection is the most plausible explanation of the Christian phenomenon in the early Christian centuries. Still a third answer is that the Christ of the Gospels is the best explanation for the mark Christianity has left in almost two thousand years of history. A fourth answer is that the deepest needs of our lives are met in Jesus Christ. (The third and fourth answers will be developed in the next chapter.)

Nothing that has been said proves beyond any doubt that the Christian view of Jesus is accurate. However, there is strong enough evidence for any open-minded seeker to consider seriously the claims of Christ. There is also confirmation enough for Christians to maintain their faith with complete intellectual integrity.

This is a strong part of Elton Trueblood's thesis in his book *A Place to Stand*. He issues a strong call for a rational approach to the evidences for Christian faith. He personally has found in Christ a "center of certitude" on which to take his stand. But Trueblood does not advocate a purely intellectual approach to Christian faith. He knows that reason alone is not enough—total commitment is needed.[18]

A. Leonard Griffith wrote a book on *Barriers to Christian Belief*. He presented a strong approach designed to help people with intellectual barriers to Christian faith. In the final chapter on "Belief Is Commitment," he writes: "The biggest obstacle to Christian belief does not lie in some thorny theological issue, nor yet in some burning practical issue, but in our own timidity and indecisiveness. If we are not Christians, it is not because our religious questions remain unanswered, but because we cannot reach a decision, we cannot make up our minds to follow Jesus Christ." [19]

Griffith is not unaware of genuine intellectual barriers to belief. After all, he wrote an entire book to help persons who struggle with such problems. His point is that because faith is basically commitment, this is the real crux of the matter. A person may examine the evidences for Christ and his way; he may find answers for many of his intellectual difficulties. Yet he may still be as far from Christ as he ever was. How can this be? Because he is unwilling to make the commitment that is involved in Christian faith.

Often a person who has had serious problems with doubt will blame his indecisiveness on his continuing doubts. Does he suppose any serious-minded person ever has all his doubts resolved or all his questions answered?

What was said at the end of chapter 1 applies even more so to distinctly Christian faith. Christian faith is not the inevitable conclusion of considering a series of reasons for believing in

Christ. However strong and convincing are the evidences for Christianity, there is always enough uncertainty and mystery (not to mention human self-will) for a faith-commitment to be necessary.

A faith-commitment tends to validate the truth of the experience. This does not mean that a Christian sees clearly everything he once doubted and questioned. No, Christians still walk by faith, not sight. Yet as we take each step in the pilgrimage of faith, we find light that is sufficient to show the way—however dimly it sometimes may be illumined.

John Bunyan's classic allegory of the Christian life, *The Pilgrim's Progress*, has stood the test of time. Bunyan's story reflects the realities of a life of Christian faith. As Christian prepared to begin his pilgrimage, he sought directions from Evangelist. "Then said Evangelist (pointing with his finger over a very wide field), 'Do you see yonder wicket gate?' The man said, 'No.' Then said the other, 'Do you see yonder shining light?' He said, 'I think I do.' " [20]

Some people wait for a clear view of the light before embarking on the path of faith. Bunyan knew better. Christian thought he could see the light; therefore, he headed toward it. He met many difficulties on his pilgrimage, but he found increasing light and confirmation for his faith as he went along.

4
How Can We Believe That Christ Offers What We Really Need?

A new family moved into the community. The members of a nearby church made several contacts with the new people in their midst. One day as the pastor of the church visited in their home, the lady of the house said: "You are a nice man. Your members are friendly people. But—to be very honest—my family and I just are not interested in religion."

This woman is typical of many to whom Christian faith and commitment are personally unimportant and unnecessary. She is willing to live in a community with churches for people who are interested in such things, but she is not personally interested. She is not a militant unbeliever; on the contrary, she professes some of the same beliefs and ideals as Christians do. However, she has no personal interest in Christianity. Her problem is not so much that she finds Christianity unbelievable but that she considers it irrelevant. After all, she wonders, what does Christianity offer that she and her family really need?

In 1952 Georgia Harkness wrote a book entitled *The Modern Rival of Christian Faith.* She identified this rival as secularism, which she defined as the organization of life as if God does not exist. A secular society need not be a society of professed atheists. Most people in our society still profess to believe in God. However, this professed belief in many cases involves no personal commitment or life-ordering relationships. The belief is irrelevant in terms of any real influence on actual values, attitudes, or actions.[1]

The assumption of the modern secular spirit is that the present generation has outgrown any need for religion. As noted in earlier chapters, a growing number of people feel we have outgrown not only any need for religion but also any possibility of belief in the claims of the Christian religion. However, the basic response of a secular society to Christianity is not unbelief but unconcern. Whether or not Christianity is believable is considered irrelevant because if Christianity is unimportant, what difference does it make whether or not you can believe it? Thus for some people Christianity is both unbelievable and irrelevant, but for many more it is simply irrelevant. They ask, What difference does it make one way or the other? Their assumption is that Christianity does not really offer anything that modern man needs. In other words, they feel that "We can get by just as well without it."

Christianity—Help or Hindrance?

Can we get along without Christianity? In one sense, this is an academic question. In a general way all of us are indirect beneficiaries of the Christian faith. Western civilization has historical Christian roots. Christianity has left its marks on our society.

It would be somewhat like a United States citizen asking, "Can I get along without freedom?" A person may or may not be committed to the principles of freedom reflected in the United States Constitution. In either case, he benefits from the heritage of freedom all of us enjoy. Even a person committed to overthrowing the government benefits from the very freedom he is opposing.

Over the centuries Christianity has exerted a good and positive influence. Its best and most fruitful impact has been in the lives of those with personal faith and commitment. However, those who have followed Christ and his way have influenced for good their families, their neighbors, and society as a whole. Where Christ and his way have been preached and practiced, individual lives and society as a whole have been changed for the better.

Critics of Christianity, of course, do not agree. In fact, some critics charge that Christianity has hurt rather than helped. This was Bertrand Russell's position. Russell spoke and wrote on the subject *Why I Am Not a Christian.* He considered Christianity not only untrue but harmful. He vigorously attacked the claim that Christianity has benefited society. To the contrary, he charged, Christianity is responsible for much of the evil in the world. Rather than promoting moral progress, Christianity has opposed and retarded progress. He pointed, for example, to such dark spots in religious history as the Inquisition. On this basis Russell wrote, "I say quite deliberately that the Christian religion, as organized in the churches, has been and still is the principal enemy of real progress in the world." [2]

Such a reading of history assumes that Christianity caused the Dark Ages and that since then Christianity has opposed every forward movement. Not everyone reads history this way. G. K. Chesterton refused to accept such sweeping assumptions: "I did not satisfy myself with reading modern generalisations; I read a little history. And in history I found that Christianity, so far from belonging to the Dark Ages, was the one path across the Dark Ages that was not dark." [3]

Of course, such things as the Inquisition are part of history. And the most predominant institutional form of Christianity in that day was largely responsible for the Inquisition. However, no one who reads the New Testament can possibly conclude that the Inquisition actually represented Christianity. What it actually represented was the same sort of ungodly religious power structure that condemned Jesus Christ to be crucified—all in the supposed name of God and goodness.

Dostoevski powerfully portrayed this in his account of the Grand Inquisition in *The Brothers Karamazov.* He imagined Jesus

Christ himself coming to earth in the days of the Inquisition. The Grand Inquisitor recognized him. The old man in the robes of the church quickly had Christ arrested. Later the Inquisitor went to the prisoner's cell and charged Christ with coming to hinder the good work of the Inquisition. Christ was told that he would be burned at the stake as the worst of all heretics.

Those who have claimed to be acting in the name of Christ have not always represented the spirit of Christ. Sometimes—as in the case of the Inquisition—they have acted in a completely contrary spirit. Some have enslaved others; some have even tortured and killed—supposedly in Christ's name.

Most fair-minded people realize that it is unfair to fault Christianity because of what such people have done. Christianity should be judged by the impact of those persons whose lives have in some measure reflected the likeness of the Christ of the Gospels. The history of Christianity is a checkered one. If a person sees only the dark spots, he may draw a conclusion similar to Russell's; but if he looks at the flashes of light, he should draw a very different conclusion.

For example, consider the impact of the evangelical revival of the eighteenth century. This historical phenomenon resulted not only in the changed lives of countless individuals but also in a positive impact on society. One of those who was changed was Ashley Cooper, Earl of Shaftesbury. He was an impassioned social reformer who vigorously attacked the evils of oppressive work conditions. He struggled on behalf of the shamefully exploited child laborers of his day. These activities grew directly out of his warmly evangelical experience with Christ.

William Wilberforce was another convert of Wesley and Whitefield's evangelical awakening. He became England's great emancipator of the slaves. Others, of course, saw no contradiction between their support of slavery and their profession of Christian faith. What is significant, however, was the deeply religious roots of those whose actions eventually destroyed slavery.

Christ did not come as a social reformer. He came as Savior from sin and Lord of new life. His initial impact was the transformation of the lives of believers. However, wherever people have taken Jesus seriously, the impact has registered on society as a whole. Jesus came as light into the ancient world. That light through him and his followers pervaded and began to change the dark, chaotic plight of humanity. This has been true whenever the gospel has been preached and believed.

Many of the good things about modern society are the results of the impact of Christianity. We all are heirs of a Christian heritage that has bequeathed to us many rich gifts.

"Uneasiness in the Brave New World"

This is the title of one of the chapters in Roger L. Shinn's book *Man: the New Humanism*. "Humanism is the appreciation of man and of the values, real and potential, in human life." [4] Humanism in the best sense of the word is compatible with the biblical nature of man—in right relation to God, others, and the created order. However, much of the humanism of the current age is only another facet of secularism. The assumption is that humanity does not need God in order to reach its full potential; on the contrary, humanity can create a brave new world.

In 1932 Aldous Huxley wrote *Brave New World*; in 1949 George Orwell wrote *Nineteen Eighty-Four*. Both writers describe a world in which man's use of science and technology has created a supposed Utopia. But the terrifying reality is that the utopia is much more of a hell than a heaven. Humanity's best-laid schemes of a brave new world have a way of turning out this way.

The claim that humanity can get along without God is an unproved assumption. In fact, believing this assumption takes a considerable leap of faith because all the evidence is against it. Such utopian schemes have a poor success rating. Those nations that have embraced communism demonstrate the end result of secular humanism. Not only Christian faith but also Christian morality have been replaced with a faith in scientific technology and a morality consistent with communism's own goals. Russia has been operating under these assumptions for over half a century, as has China for over a quarter of a century. Yet neither of these nations is a showcase for the brave new world of secular humanism. To the contrary, both societies bear frightening resemblances to the Utopias of Huxley and Orwell. Some naive observers are impressed by that which they are allowed to see of communist society. This is particularly true nowadays of some glowing reports from China. Yet even these reports of an ordered, almost crime-free society bear marked resemblances to the outward order in *Brave New World*. The outward order has been achieved at the cost of human freedom.

Thus intelligent people always have a sense of uneasiness about the rosy forecasts of secular humanists. There is a sense of unreality in the easy assumption of those who believe that modern people have outgrown any need for Christian faith and commitment. Such people seem blissfully unaware of the benefits they already have received from a Christian heritage. They also seem unaware of the dangers of a society with a Christian heritage cutting itself off from its own moral and spiritual roots.

In 1944 Elton Trueblood wrote a book called *The Predicament of Modern Man*. This was a short but penetrating essay on the breakdown and potential for restoration in western civilization. Three decades later in his autobiography Trueblood quoted again the key passage from *The Predicament of Modern Man:*

> The terrible danger of our time consists in the fact that ours is a *cut-flower civilization*. Beautiful as cut flowers may be, and much as we may use our ingenuity to keep them looking fresh for a while, they will eventually die, and they die because they are severed from their sustaining roots. We are trying to maintain

the dignity of the individual apart from the deep faith that every man is made in God's image and is therefore precious in God's eyes.[5]

This simple analogy of the cut flowers is a graphic and accurate picture of the plight of modern society. Western civilization has deep roots in the Christian faith. Large segments of our society have embraced secularism and cut themselves off from their spiritual roots. Many people naively assume that we can continue to uphold the moral standards of Christianity even though we have detached ourselves from the spiritual roots of Christian morality. We can no more do this successfully than a cut flower can continue to bloom. The cut flower can maintain its bloom for a while—under some conditions longer than others—but eventually the bloom will wilt, then wither and die.

This is not to say that no individual can live a moral life without maintaining the spiritual roots of Christian morality. Many secular humanists are people of high ethical standards. The question, however, is whether or not succeeding generations can maintain Christian standards of morality without Christian faith and commitment. Many well-intentioned people maintain that morality can be based on purely humanistic foundations. Others of us are not convinced that this is so.

Are there not strong evidences that the bloom is already wilting? One does not need to be an especially astute observer to recognize symptoms of moral decay in the modern scene. George Buttrick writes:

> How can anyone intelligently say that modern man has outgrown the need for God? Or even proclaim that we are 'getting along very well' without God? Our industry lives with a gaping lesion: the strife between labor and capital. Our politics breed wars that may destroy the whole world. Our culture is a hideous contrast between slums and suburbs, and between race and race. Violence makes our streets unsafe, and nervous ills multi-

ply. 'Getting along' is precisely what we are not doing: we are falling apart—for lack of a creative faith.[6]

What then can we say about the assumption that modern man has outgrown any need for Christian faith and commitment? We have seen that it is an unrealistic assumption. The dream of a brave new world turns out to be a nightmare.

And it is not only unrealistic but also arrogant to claim that modern man is all that different from preceding generations. Many secular humanists will actually say something like this: "Christian faith was all right for earlier generations. They were able to believe it because they were not so well-informed as we. And they found some supposed help in its promises of divine strength in times of need. However, we have outgrown all that. We can no longer believe it, and besides we no longer need it."

According to Elton Trueblood, one of the reigning tenets of our times is the disease of contemporaneity. Modern humanity has a condescending indifference about the past and a haughty superiority about the present. This view discounts the contributions of the past and a modern person's continuing need for some of the lasting values of the past. In terms of our Christian heritage, the disease of contemporaneity "means that we cut ourselves off from the wisdom of the ages, including that of the Bible. It means that, if this is taken seriously, we are really an orphan generation—an orphan generation that takes itself far too seriously, that is too much impressed with changes that may be only superficial." [7]

Leslie Weatherhead said that "the curse of modern life is man's decision that God does not matter, that man can manage, that man is the master of things." He illustrated this with

> the old Danish fable which tells how a spider slid down a single filament of web from the lofty timbers of a beam and established himself on a lower level. There he spread his web, caught flies, grew sleek and prospered. One Sunday afternoon, wandering about his premises, he saw the thread that stretched up into the

dark unseen above him, and thought, "How useless!" He snapped it. *But his web collapsed* and soon was trodden under foot.[8]

The Forgiveness of Sins

In 1962 Jerome Hines was on a concert tour in the Soviet Union. He sought opportunity of bearing witness to Jesus Christ. At the climax of his Moscow tour he sang the title role of *Boris Godunov* before a Bolstoi Theater audience that included Premier Khrushchev. At the end of the opera Boris exclaims, "Forgive me, Forgive me"; then he falls dead. When Hines came to that part of the opera, he changed the wording slightly but significantly to "Oh, my God, forgive me." He thus was able to bear witness to his faith that it is God who forgives our sins.

Thus far in this chapter we have been looking at the influence of Christianity on society as a whole. Now we turn to the more personal dimension of Christian faith and commitment. The chapter title asks, "How can we believe that Christ offers what we really need?" One thing it offers is forgiveness of sins. The Christian religion teaches that we are sinners who need forgiveness and that God in Christ offers forgiveness and new life.

Many people do not get beyond the first part of the last statement. They never take seriously Christ's forgiveness because they do not take seriously the biblical assumption of human sinfulness. The ideas of sin and guilt sound old-fashioned and outmoded to many modern ears. These are viewed as carry-overs from the days of "hellfire and damnation" sermons: Sin and guilt were acceptable ideas for our Puritan ancestors, but we have moved beyond such archaic concepts.

Karl Menninger has written a probing analysis of this outlook in his book *Whatever Became of Sin?* This noted psychiatrist points out that the word *sin* has disappeared from public use: The only wrong behavior that deserves attention is crime, which calls for imprisonment, or disease, which calls for treatment. But apart from these categories the ways we act are neither sinful nor immoral.

Menninger believes that trying to explain away sin has had harmful effects on individuals and on society itself. He writes:

> I believe there is "sin" which is expressed in ways which cannot be subsumed under verbal artifacts such as "crime," "disease," "delinquent," "deviancy." There *is* immorality; there *is* unethical behavior; there *is* wrongdoing. And I hope to show that there is usefulness of retaining the concept, and indeed the word, SIN, which now shows some signs of returning to public acceptance. I would like to help this trend along.[9]

As a psychiatrist Menninger has given his life to help sick people. Thus he acknowledges that he expects many to be surprised by his attempt to focus attention on the reality of sin, guilt, and personal responsibility. However, he does not see this as a backward but as a forward move. He certainly does not intend to deny the positive benefits of his own field of psychology in helping to treat emotional illness. However, he believes that acknowledging and confessing sin and guilt bring positive benefits to all of us and open new possibilities of treating some forms of neuroses.

Menninger believes that a renewed sense of personal accountability for our own actions is essential for healthy lives and a healthy society. And the acknowledgment and confession of sin and guilt is an essential part of accepting responsibility for our own actions. As we face up to our own sins we will be able to find release from guilt and a foundation for acting more responsibly in the future. This lies at the very heart of Christianity. The New Testament presents Jesus Christ as the Savior for sinners. One of the early Christian symbols was the fish. The Greek word for fish had five letters—each of which was the first letter in the Greek words for this confession: Jesus Christ God's Son Savior.

The cross has become the chief symbol of Christianity. The New

Testament sees the cross as the meeting place between man's sin and God's love. Paul wrote that "God was in Christ reconciling the world to himself" (2 Cor. 5:19). God in Christ absorbed the evil and hurt of human sin and guilt; and on that basis of suffering, atoning love offers forgiveness to sinners.

E. Stanley Jones told of a man who had been unfaithful to his marriage vows. Even though the adulterous relationship was over, he felt a heavy burden of guilt because he had betrayed the loyal love and trust of his wife. One day he tried to unburden his soul of guilt by confessing to his wife what he had done. As the meaning of his words dawned on her, she turned pale and began to weep. The guilty man could see the anguish that she must have felt. Finally when she was able to speak she assured him of her continued love for him and of her willingness to forgive what he had done. The man was deeply moved. He said later: "In that moment I saw the meaning of the cross. I saw love crucified by sin."

True forgiveness always is costly. The one who forgives pays the cost by absorbing the hurt that has been done. On a cosmic scale, that is what God in Christ did at the cross. His suffering love absorbed the deadly hurt of humanity's sin.

How desperately we all need such forgiveness. We may try to deny or to ignore our guilt. Or we may simply say, "There's no use crying over spilt milk; I'll do better the next time." But none of these approaches really come to grips with the seriousness of our moral accountability. Sin and guilt are real and deadly. However, the Christian gospel (good news) is that God in Christ is able to forgive our sin and to give us new life.

Search for Meaning

Dag Hammarskjöld served as secretary general of the United Nations during a tense and crucial period in world history. He kept a kind of journal or diary, which was published after his death. Surprisingly, the diary makes no reference to the famous people he met or to the significant events in which he played such an important role. Instead, the diary records the inner life of a man. Hammarskjöld referred to the diary *"as a sort of white book concerning my negotiations with myself—and with God.*[10]

Markings records the spiritual pilgrimage of a modern man who sought and found something very precious—meaning. One of the entries, dated 1952, reflects his earnest quest:

> What I ask for is absurd: that life shall have a meaning.
> What I strive for is impossible: that my life shall acquire a meaning.
> I dare not believe, I do not see how I shall ever be able to believe: that I am not alone.[11]

A later entry records this significant entry:

> I don't know Who—or what—put the question, I don't know when it was put. I don't even remember answering. But at some moment I did answer *Yes* to Someone—or Something—and from that hour I was certain that existence is meaningful and that, therefore, my life, in self-surrender, had a goal.[12]

Although Hammarskjöld used terms that sound somewhat vague ("Someone—or Something"), in the same entry he showed clearly that he was writing of Jesus Christ and his "Way," the way of the cross.

The human quest for meaning reflects a basic need. Viktor E. Frankl has based his approach to psychotherapy on this primary force in life. He calls his approach *logotherapy*, which he explains as follows:

> *Logos* is a Greek word that denotes "meaning." Logotherapy . . . focuses on the meaning of human existence as well as on man's search for such a meaning. According to logotherapy, this striving to find meaning in one's life is the primary motivational force in man. That is why I speak of a *will to meaning* in contrast to the pleasure principle (or, as we could also term it, the *will to pleasure*) on which Freudian psychoanalysis is centered, as well

in contrast to the *will to power* stressed by Adlerian psychology.[13]

Frankl's theory is rooted in his own personal experience as a survivor of the Nazi concentration camps. Part 1 of the book *Man's Search for Meaning: an Introduction to Logotherapy* is an account of his experiences during that ordeal. He was subjected to the most dehumanizing conditions imaginable—stripped not only of all his possessions but also of his name. He was forced to work under terrible conditions by brutal captors. As time passed he began to analyze why some prisoners survived under such conditions. He discovered that a sense of meaning was an important factor. Under those terrible conditions many despaired of life, meaning, hope—they lost the will to live and they died. But others managed to find meaning—usually some sense of inner meaning. Many found it in religious faith; others, in a task yet unfinished; still others, in the sustaining memories of family and friends and in the possibility of reunion with them.

Apathy was the natural state of persons subjected to the endless brutality of prison life—apathy about anything or anyone. Some, however, were able to find meaning in their suffering. When stripped of everything but suffering, they found meaning in that suffering—as theirs to bear and to bear as nobly and courageously as possible. They refused to be robbed of their humanity—their freedom under the worst of conditions to make their own response to the situation.

Few of us will argue with Frankl's basic thesis that meaning is an inherent need for human beings. This is completely compatible with the biblical view of man as a creature made in God's image—a being with a moral and spiritual dimension to his existence. However, the Bible stresses that human beings need more than meaning; we need *ultimate* meaning. We need more than a purpose in life; we need a purpose for life as a whole. According to the biblical view we find meaning in commonplace things such as

How Can We Believe that Christ Offers What We Really Need?

work, play, marriage, parenthood, friendship, and even suffering because life itself is seen in the context of God's larger purpose. This ultimate purpose, which comes from commitment to God's will, gives meaning to life as a whole and to the commonplace events of life.

Over against this view stand those who represent two contrasting points of view. One group assumes that a satisfying meaning to life can be found apart from any ultimate meaning. The other group despairs of finding any satisfying meaning either commonplace or ultimate. To the latter group life itself is inherently absurd and meaningless; thus, the best we can do is to go on with life in spite of its basic meaninglessness.

Langdon Gilkey gives this description of those who hold the former view:

> Most young Americans begin life with unexplored and uncomplicated assumptions of human meaning. From their culture they have absorbed a few rather simple goals in life, things which they take for granted are essential for fulfillment and happiness. They hope to find a job that will be creative, and that will bring them increasing economic security, physical comfort, and social prestige. They expect to have a home and friends that will provide love and warm associations; and they anticipate leisure time for pleasant diversions such as fishing, boating, or golf.[14]

This naive view of meaning overlooks two crucial facts: the nature of human existence and the nature of human beings. The realities of human existence often seem to work against attaining even the simplest of goals. All sorts of things can interfere with goals related to health, home, work, and success. We must take into account such realities as illness, injuries, death, economic reverses, and so forth. As people grow older, they become increasingly aware of the brevity and uncertainty of human existence.

Yet even when conditions allow us to attain the goals we seek, we need to take account of something more basic to our nature than the satisfaction of attaining commonplace goals. By our very natures as human beings, we need some meaning beyond ourselves. This explains why many people are haunted by feelings of emptiness even when they have attained all their goals.

One day late in his life Clarence Darrow, the famous criminal lawyer, asked a Christian friend, "Would you like to know my favorite Bible verse?" When the friend expressed interest Darrow said: "You'll find it in Luke 5:5—'We have toiled all the night, and have taken nothing' [KJV]. In spite of my successes that verse seems to sum up the way I feel about my life."

A graphic symbol of this emptiness is a small machine on an executive's desk. It is a small wooden casket with a switch on one side. When the switch is pushed, a buzzer sounds, the lid of the casket raises, and a hand emerges. The hand turns off the switch. The hand goes back inside the casket, the lid is closed, and the buzzing ceases.

These two factors—the nature of human existence and the nature of human beings—account for the view of those who despair of finding any meaning in life. Their basic premise is that life is inherently absurd. The view that life is meaningless is expressed in many of the art forms of our day—art, music, novels, and plays. Over and over the point is made that there is no point.

None of this should be surprising to those familiar with the Christian religion. The Bible teaches that apart from the ultimate meaning of God's will, human life and existence become meaningless. However, Christ calls us to a way that gives meaning to the commonplace because of the ultimate meaning found in following him. He calls us to follow him in the way of the cross and resurrection. A commitment to him involves a personal relationship with him who died and was raised. Christ enables us to follow him in a way that brings self-fulfillment as a person lives in proper relation to God and others. He has a relationship to the eternal God, our heavenly Father. The life of the believer contributes to the vast, ongoing purpose of God.

Unbelievers often do not see how such a way is meaningful. The cross was a stumbling block in its day, and it still is. Persons who measure life by the criteria of pleasure, profit, and prestige cannot see how self-giving, especially self-giving that involves sacrifice and even suffering, can give meaning and satisfaction. They cannot understand either Jesus' life or his teachings. They are stumped by such profound paradoxes as these: "Blessed are the meek, for they shall inherit the earth" (Matt. 5:5). "If any man would come after me, let him deny himself and take up his cross daily and follow me. For whoever would save his life will lose it; and whoever loses his life for my sake, he will save it" (Luke 9:23–24).

One popular explanation for religious faith is that it is a wish projection. The nineteenth-century philosopher Feuerbach taught that the gods humans worship and pray to are only the projections of their own wishes. Sigmund Freud also used this theory to explain what seemed to him the strange persistence of religious faith. According to this view, the stresses of human existence cause many people to wish for some divine Father-figure to whom they can turn for strength and help.

There is enough truth in some of these premises to make this a popular resort of those who prefer to think of Christianity as a delusion. Man's plight is hard, and God in Christ does offer strength and help. However, although this theory explains some of the facts, it fails to explain others. Christ and his way provide comfort, help, and hope; but Christ also calls us to commitment—total commitment to the way of self-giving love. The unavoidable question is this: If God is only a "wish-projection," why did humans dream up a God who builds a Calvary and calls us to walk in that way?

The wish-projection for a Father-figure cannot explain either this biblical challenge or why people continue to respond to the challenge.

Yet followers of Christ understand. Hammarskjöld made this discovery. When the diary of his spiritual pilgrimage is laid alongside his life, we realize that he found meaning not in his position and fame but in the way he lived, served, and died as a follower of Christ.

Life's Dead Ends

The woman mentioned at the beginning of this chapter assumed that Christianity offered nothing she and her family really needed. We already have seen two things Christ offers that they really need—forgiveness and meaning. Now we will look at a third thing—hope.

Hope, of course, is closely related to forgiveness and meaning. In fact, all three of these are interrelated and interdependent. Meaning and hope flow out of forgiveness. And there can be no ultimate meaning without hope. These three focus on what Christianity offers in relation to past, present, and future. Christ gives forgiveness, which looses us from the past with its burdens and chains of guilt. Christianity gives meaning for daily living in the present. Christianity gives hope as we anticipate what lies in the future.

To say that hope is essential to life is a truism. This is so obvious that it needs little demonstration. The sayings and writings of all cultures are filled with words that bear out this fact. And each of us knows from experience that this is so.

One proverb common to many authors is "Where there's life, there's hope." Karl Menninger maintains that the opposite is even more true. The thesis of his book *The Vital Balance* is "that life is sustained by hope—that where there is hope there is life." [15] Hope is not the only stance from which to face the future. Anxiety, fear, and despair are other possibilities; however, hope is the only outlook that makes life worth living. When hope is gone, people usually die. Even when physical life goes on, meaning and joy end—and one is not living, just existing. The ancient Greeks used the word *hope* in two ways. Some writers spoke of hope in a bright optimistic tone; others were cynical about hope. The latter group charged that hope was a deceitful goddess luring men on to ruin with false promises of a brighter tomorrow. People hope for health and get illness. They hope for success and get failure, for love and get indifference, for joy and get misery, for meaning and get tedium, for long life and get death.

No matter what way we choose, life seems to lead us eventually to some dead end. Some cold reality puts an end to our dreams. Today is unbearable and tomorrow—if there be a tomorrow—offers only more of the same. We do not know whether we can go on living or even if we want to under such conditions.

Christian hope is not some bright, naively optimistic forecast of the future. To the contrary, it grows out of the soil of suffering and death. The cross stands as a stark reminder of the reality of sin, suffering, and death. However, Christian hope declares that these dark enemies do not have the final word. The crucifixion is not God's final word; the resurrection puts the crucifixion in totally new perspective. The realities of sin, suffering, and death are not denied; instead, they are overcome by God's grace and power. The resurrection declares that real though they are, sin, suffering, and death do not have the last word.

More will be said in chapter 6 about the reasons for Christian hope in life after death. The emphasis here is on the impact of this hope on present attitudes and actions. Christian hope is not a detached and irrelevant belief in a life after death. It is a commitment that transcends and pervades all of life. The biblical hope of eternal life is not focused on the individual's survival after death; it is focused on the shared life of those who are caught up in God's larger purpose.

Such hope has power to sustain Christians when they face the dead ends of life. It sustains with the promise that there is a way beyond what seems to be and often is an end to part of life. It also sustains with the assurance that as we await that way beyond, our actions serve some larger purpose. We usually cannot fathom that purpose, but we believe it is there.

George Buttrick writes:

> My students are fond of telling how the Sea of Galilee has clear water because the River Jordan flows through it, whereas the Dead Sea is dead because it has no exit. The parable flatters our activisms. But the Dead Sea does have an exit—upward. It surrenders to the burning sky. Therefore, the scientists tell us, there are deposits of potash around its shores, enough to fertilize all earth's fields for five centuries.[16]

Jean-Paul Sartre, the French existentialist, wrote a play called "No Exit." He tells of three evil people who have died and who find themselves together in a room with no windows. They realize they are in hell but at first are relieved that there are no torturers with burning coals. But as time passes, they realize that they are one another's torturers. These three are doomed to be forever in that one room with one another. In a frenzy one grabs a paper knife and stabs another. But nothing happens. They are in the ultimate "no exit" situation.

By contrast Christ promises that no dead end is final for those who follow him. There is always a way beyond. He is Lord of past, present, and future. With him there is always a future, a tomorrow—and the ultimate tomorrow is bright with hope.

The Evidence of Experience

G. K. Chesterton was a confirmed unbeliever who became a committed Christian. He said that what first aroused his interest in Christianity were the attacks of its critics. These attacks were so intense and so diverse that he became convinced that Christianity was something extraordinary, to say the least.

Chesterton was impressed by the fact that "it was attacked on all sides and for all contradictory reasons." [17] Christianity was attacked by one critic as too pessimistic and by another as too optimistic. Or it was attacked as too warlike on one hand and too meek on the other. Or it was said to be too narrow by one group and too broad by another. And so on. At first Chesterton only concluded that Christianity must be a most extraordinary evil. But then one day another possibility occurred to him:

> Suppose we heard an unknown man spoken of by many men. Suppose we were puzzled to hear that some men said he was too tall and some too short; some objected to his fatness, some lamented his leanness; some thought him too dark, and some too fair. One explanation . . . would be that he might be an odd shape. But there is another explanation. He might be the right shape. Outrageously tall men might feel him to be short. Very short men might feel him to be tall. Old bucks who are growing stout might consider him insufficiently filled out; old beaux who are growing thin might feel that he expanded the narrow lines of elegance. Perhaps Swedes (who have pale hair like tow) called him a dark man, while negroes considered him distinctly blond. Perhaps (in short) this extraordinary thing is really the ordinary thing; at least the normal thing, the centre. Perhaps after all, it is Christianity that is sane and all its critics that are mad—in various ways.[18]

Chesterton is right: Christ and his way are often criticized and misunderstood. Yet the problem is not in Christianity but in the critics. Some people judge the Christ of the New Testament by their own narrow presuppositions. On that basis they conclude they cannot believe. What they fail to see is that although Christ and the Christian way do not fit into their own way of thinking, they do fit reality—reality as attested to by history and by human experience. As C. S. Lewis noted, Christ is like the central part of a novel or the main theme of a symphony, which gives meaning to the whole.

Many in today's society are like the woman mentioned at the beginning of this chapter: They feel no need for Christ and his way.

They feel they are beyond needing what others in earlier generations found through Christian faith and commitment. The thesis of this chapter has been that this dismissal is based on a superficial view not only of Christ but also of ourselves. The Christian life is as up to date and vital today as it has always been. With all our modern attainments we still need those things that Christ offers—forgiveness, meaning, hope.

Those who have taken the leap of faith and embarked on the Christian pilgrimage have the strongest of all validations of Christianity—the evidence of personal experience. We know the One who forgives our sin and imparts the power of a new life, who gives meaning to life as a whole and to its separate parts, who assures us that there is always a future for those who follow him. All this and far more!

5
How Can We Believe That God Really Answers Prayer?

A British soldier returned to his family after fighting in World War I. His family told him that they had been sure he would come back because they had prayed for him. He protested bitterly: "Don't talk like that! I cannot bear it! It is just chance who comes back and who dies. I prayed for people in the war who have been killed!" He told of a group of British soldiers who were retreating under heavy enemy fire. They had reached a tiny thicket that provided a little cover. Then the scrub caught fire, and the men were burned to death. All the while their comrades had been praying for them—first for their safety, then for a mercifully quick death. Neither prayer was answered. The bitter veteran said to his family: "What is the use of telling me that you protected me by your prayers? How could we have been protected when the other men were left to burn to death? We prayed with passion, with madness, and we were not heard." [1]

Eddie Rickenbacker was forced to make a crash landing in the Pacific during World War II. He and seven others were set adrift on three small rubber rafts. They had no water, and their only food was four small oranges. They had fishhooks but no bait. They ate the last orange on the sixth day. One man had a New Testament. Rickenbacker suggested morning and evening prayer meetings. Each man read a Bible passage, and one of them would pray. On the eighth day after the prayers a sea gull landed on Rickenbacker's

83

hat. They ate the bird and used his intestines as bait to catch fish. That night it rained, and they had water for the first time in eight days. They hoarded all they could for later use. And they needed it during the twenty-four long days and nights before rescue. With this sustenance and water from a few other showers, seven of the eight survived the ordeal. Of the sea gull Rickenbacker wrote: "Some may call it a coincidence. I call it a gift from heaven." [2] He considered their survival an evidence that God has answered their prayers.

On the basis of his experience the British soldier believed that God does not answer prayer. By contrast, Rickenbacker was strongly convinced that God does answer prayer.

Once again we are confronted by an issue that cannot be proved one way or the other. Faith is the crucial factor: A person either believes in prayer or he does not believe. His experience will be a strong factor, yet not the determining factor. Many people have had experiences similar to the British soldier's; yet they still believe in prayer. Likewise, many have had experiences somewhat like Rickenbacker's; yet they chalk it all up to coincidence, not to answered prayer.

Therefore, my goal in this chapter is not to *prove* that God really answers prayer. Rather, I hope to state what Christians mean by this claim and to give evidence to support the claim. Although the evidence will not prove the case, it hopefully will show that the Christian belief in God answering prayer is not unreasonable.

Prayer is not a side issue in Christian faith. Rather, it is at the heart of the matter. If God does not hear and answer prayer, faith in a personal God (as in Christianity) is a delusion. God is either nonexistent or he is at best only an impersonal force. On the other hand, if God does hear and answer prayer, there is every reason to believe the other claims of personal religion.

Prayer by George A. Buttrick is probably the most helpful book on the subject. He writes: "Perhaps our scientific agnosticism knows, though dimly, that if prayer can be riddled by argument or captured by scoffing the whole realm of religion will fall. Perhaps the badly shaken forces of religion also know, though dimly, that if prayer is renewed the prevalent scepticism must bow." [3]

Why Do So Many People Pray?

The persistent, widespread practice of prayer is a phenomenon that cannot be ignored. Throughout human history people have prayed. Even today, when skeptics say scientific knowledge has destroyed the basis for prayer, people still pray.

Some pray daily because for them prayer is as natural as breathing. Others pray only when life's crises threaten to overwhelm them. Some pray because they have a strong, carefully thought-out faith that God, our heavenly Father, hears and answers prayer. Others pray out of an innate sense of need for help and guidance from someone beyond the human realm.

The wide diversity of persons who pray is striking. Some are like Daniel who "got down upon his knees three times a day and prayed and gave thanks before his God" (Dan. 6:10). He even continued to do so when he knew that such praying could result in his arrest and execution. Others who pray are nominal believers or even unbelievers. Ordinarily they ignore God and prayer, but then in some extreme situation they cry out to God for help. Or in the midst of some great joy they feel the need to express thanks to something beyond themselves.

Some of this latter group later repent of their prayers. Some, like the soldier who prayed for his comrades, bitterly deny that God answers prayer. Still, he and the others prayed. Why should he have even thought of praying? If nothing else, his praying attests to the persistence of the human belief that prayer is at least one possible response to crisis.

In his book *The Meaning of Prayer* Harry Emerson Fosdick wrote that "praying is first of all a native tendency. It is a practice like breathing or eating in this respect, that men engage in because they are human, and afterward argue about it as best they can."[4]

Lawrence M. Brings edited a book called *We Believe in Prayer*. In the introduction he explains how the book came to be:

> I decided to poll certain leaders of America and of the world, asking them to express their views about the value and efficacy of prayer based upon their own experience and observation. No attempt was made to ascertain their religious or denominational background, or even to select individuals from whom I might expect a favorable reply. Frankly, I informed them that I had nothing to offer them except their personal satisfaction in contributing an article to this book *We Believe in Prayer*.
>
> Letters were sent to hundreds of topflight people in many diversified areas of human endeavor. The response was overwhelming. I was surprised that so many persons occupying positions of achievement and responsibility would take the time to write a special statement for this book, giving their personal testimony about the power of prayer as experienced by them. In this book you will find proof that prayer is a potent force in the lives of thousands of our leaders.[5]

How are we to explain this phenomenon? Could this many people be wrong? Perhaps. Maybe their praying is only a lingering residue of an earlier, more superstitious age of humankind. On the other hand, maybe they are not wrong. Perhaps their praying matches a deep innate reality about God, persons, and life.

Fosdick gave strong expression to this latter view:

> Can it be that all men, in all ages and in all lands, have been engaged in "talking to a silent world from which no answer comes"? If we can be sure of anything, is it not this—that wherever a human function has persisted, unwearied by time, uncrushed by disappointment, rising to noblest form and finest use in the noblest and finest souls, that function corresponds with some reality.[6]

The Problem of Unanswered Prayer

Since the Bible is the chief document of the Christian faith, its

How Can We Believe that God Really Answers Prayers?

testimony is important. Surprisingly, at least to those unfamiliar with its contents, the Bible gives a mixed report on the subject of answers to prayer. On the one hand, the Bible records many promises about prayer and many reports of prayers that were answered. However, the Bible also frankly acknowledges that all prayers are not answered and cites several notable examples of unanswered prayers.

Moses, for example, prayed that he might enter the Promised Land of Canaan, but his request was refused (Deut. 3:23–26). David asked the Lord to let him erect the Temple, but the job was given to his son (1 Chron. 22:7–10). The prophets prayed for the repentance of Israel and Judah, but both nations were destroyed because of their impenitence. Paul prayed three times for the removal of a "thorn in the flesh," but the thorn remained (2 Cor. 12:7–9). Jesus asked that the cup of suffering and death might be removed, but it was not (Mark 14:36). Unanswered prayers are seldom easy to explain. Nor were they easy for Bible personalities either to explain or accept. Many of these people frankly presented to God the issue of unanswered prayers. The writer of Lamentations wrote:

> Thou hast wrapped thyself with a cloud
> So that no prayer can pass through (Lam. 3:44).

Habakkuk asked:

> O Lord, how long shall I cry for help,
> and thou wilt not hear? (Hab. 1:2).

Some of the examples of unanswered prayers in the Bible were not really prayers in the highest and best sense. But others were sincere prayers by people of genuine faith and piety.

The latter category is the really crucial one; however, before turning to it, we should at least note what kinds of "prayers" are not valid prayers at all. For example, the Bible teaches that God will not answer the prayers of persons who are either hypocritical or who are clinging to unconfessed sins. Isaiah 1:15 records this strong divine word to the hypocritical worshipers of Judah:

> When you spread forth your hands,
>   I will hide my eyes from you;
> Even though you make many prayers,
>   I will not listen;
> Your hands are full of blood.

Likewise, the psalmist rejoiced in God's help but acknowledged:

> If I had cherished iniquity in my heart,
>   the Lord would not have listened (66:18).

Few people have any problems understanding why such prayers are not heard. The Bible portrays God as eager to answer prayers of sincere repentance, but the Lord does not answer the prayers of those who have no intention of turning from what is evil and destructive to themselves and others. The basic problem with such prayers is that they are not real. There is a quality of make-believe and pretense about them. The same is true of such prayers as that in Jesus' parable of the Pharisee and the publican. The Pharisee prayed not to God but "with himself" (Luke 18:11). He only went through the motions of praying.

A similar unreality marks the prayers of those who repeat words and phrases over and over—assuming that the repetition of the right words ensures divine attention. Jesus warned that such prayers merely "heap up empty phrases" (Matt. 6:7).

Some prayers are unreal because they do not represent something we earnestly desire. Fosdick pointed out that real prayer should represent a dominant desire. *"Our prayers are often unreal because they do not represent what in our inward hearts we sincerely crave."* [7]

A small boy was being tucked in for the night by his father. The child had said his bedtime prayers and presumably was ready for sleep. He had been accustomed to sleeping with a light on in his room. On this night his father informed him that he was old enough to sleep in the dark. The boy argued, but his father stood his ground. Finally, when the child realized he would soon be left alone in a dark room, he asked, "Dad, can I say my prayers again—this time more carefully?"

Jesus told two parables that teach importunity in prayer—the friend at midnight (Luke 11:5–8) and the unjust judge (Luke 18:1–5). The point is not that God is like the reluctant friend or the unjust judge. The point is that real prayer is like the earnest entreaties of the man seeking bread and the widow seeking vindication. Real prayer is earnest and persistent precisely because it is a dominant desire. Thus some prayers never rank as real prayers at all.

And what about selfish praying? James 4:2–3 identifies the two chief faults of the prayer life of many people—prayerlessness and selfish petitions: "You do not have because you do not ask. You ask and do not receive, because you ask wrongly, to spend it on your own passions." The Bible clearly encourages us to make petition a part of our prayers, but we are warned that purely selfish petitions are not answered.

A popular fallacy about prayer assumes that prayer is only petition and that a person can ask God for whatever he wants—particularly if it is something he cannot get any other way. Thus prayer becomes a kind of blank check that a person fills out to suit himself. God's only job is to cash it. Or to use another analogy, God becomes a genie who grants our every wish.

Mark Twain let Huckleberry Finn express the inevitable disillusionment that comes to those who share this view:

> Then Miss Watson she took me in the closet and prayed, but nothing come of it. She told me to pray every day, and whatever I asked for I would get it. But it warn't so. I tried it. Once I got a fish-line, but no hooks. It wasn't any good to me without hooks. I

tried for hooks three or four times, but somehow I couldn't make it work. . . .

I set down one time back in the woods and had a long think about it. I says to myself, if a body can get anything they pray for, why don't Deacon Winn get back the money he lost on pork? Why can't the widow get back her silver snuff-box that was stole? Why can't Miss Watson fat up? No, says I to myself, there ain't nothing in it.[8]

The point is not that we never should ask for material things. Jesus taught us to pray for such things but to do so in the context of trust and commitment. God is our loving Father, not a magic genie. We trust in God to give us what we need, which is not always exactly what we ask (Luke 11:11–13). We also pray in a spirit of commitment to God and his will.

Can God Do Anything?

We have been looking at that category of unanswered prayers which can be explained by something lacking in the prayer or in the person praying. But what about those unanswered prayers that are real prayers by trusting, committed people? How do we explain these? Suppose we begin by frankly admitting that all of these cannot be explained. However, there are some factors that provide help in some instances of unanswered prayers.

Can God do anything? We dealt with this question in chapter 2. At that time we were thinking about the problem of suffering. One factor, we noticed, is that we should not define the word *almighty* as if God can do anything. God is almighty, but he has chosen to limit himself in some ways—notably in connection with human freedom and the basic orderliness of his universe. God does not violate human freedom; nor does he destroy the basic fabric of nature's workings. These two self-imposed limitations are factors in some prayers that are not answered.

Consider a mother's prayer for a wayward son. The son persists in his waywardness; he does not repent. Does this mean that God has not heard the prayer? No, it means that the son has resisted all his mother's efforts and all the promptings of God toward a better life. Assuming that she has done all that she can do—in prayer and action—God also may have done all that he is going to do! He will not violate the sanctity of the human will. He will entreat and convict, but he will not storm the inner citadel into the son's will. A human being has this terrible God-given freedom, which even God will not violate. A person can reject God and good. He must live with the consequences of his choices, but no one can force him to change. Even God has chosen to limit himself to changing lives only when the persons involved want their lives to be changed.

This realization not only helps one understand why some intercessions seem to go unheard but also alleviates the fear some people have that intercession violates human freedom. What right have I to pray for another? Why should I impose on him my own idea of what he needs?

I need not worry. Nothing will be *imposed* on him. And God our Father (mine and his) will use my intercessions to call him toward what he really needs (whether or not this is what I have asked God to give him).

The basic orderliness of the created universe is another factor in many unanswered prayers. Some refer to this as natural law; George Buttrick has a better term, "cosmic faithfulness." [9]

There is a story about a girl who was asked on a geography test, "What is the highest mountain in the world?" She wrote, "Lookout Mountain." Later that day, having discovered her error, she prayed, "Oh, God, please make Lookout Mountain the highest mountain in the world." Perhaps someone had taught her that God can do anything and she was merely following through with this. Her assumption, of course, was wrong. In one sense God can do anything; but God has limited himself by his cosmic faithfulness, and he has done so because of his love for humanity. What chaos would result without cosmic faithfulness!

Henry Wadsworth Longfellow said: "What discord we should bring into the universe if our prayers were all answered! Then we should govern the world and not God. And do you think we should govern it better?" [10] However, we must be careful not to overstate this point. Otherwise we shall actually destroy any basis for answers to prayers that call for changes in circumstances or in other persons. An overstatement of this point is in fact the principal intellectual barrier to faith that God can answer such prayers.

A basic assumption of many persons raised on the scientific method is that the universe is governed by a system of wholly impersonal natural laws. A rigid system of scientific naturalism rules out any personal divine intervention. God, if there be a God, may have made the natural laws; but in any case the universe is governed by the laws of nature.

Naturalism was discussed in chapter 3 in connection with miracles. We noted then that a thoroughgoing system of naturalism, which is what consistency requires, tends to prejudge the conclusion by refusing to consider certain kinds of evidence. Every phenomenon is forced to conform to predetermined assumptions about what is possible and what is not possible. Rigid naturalism makes stronger claims for natural law than many scientists do. Science notes certain observable patterns in nature; therefore, science assumes a basic uniformity of nature. Many modern scientists, however, are not dogmatic about ruling out the possibility of occasional events that do not fit the usual patterns.

This outlook is compatible with the Christian view of prayer. This view assumes a basic orderliness in nature, but it also assumes that God is able to work within his universe to carry out his purpose.

A central purpose of George A. Buttrick's book *Prayer* is to refute a rigid view of natural law and to establish a strong probability for the view that God is active in the world and in human lives. As we have seen, Buttrick supports the idea that there is a basic uniformity in nature. He sees this cosmic faithfulness as one evidence of God's goodness and love. However, he also sees certain surprises in nature which testify to God's goodness as well as to his power.

One line of argument is to point out that if persons manipulate the supposed fixed natural laws, how much more can God do so?

> We design houses, and in them make water run uphill. We reforest to enrich the soil. We build dams to control irrigation. We remove a diseased appendix . . . . We turn the onset of death. The story of civilization is the record of the world challenging man, and man wrestling with the world to bend it to his will . . . . The real issue then is this: Is the universe, so faithful to God and men, and so pliable under man's hand, *open also to the controlling act of God?* [11]

Neither God nor man is imprisoned in a universe of fixed natural law. The actions and prayers of humanity in cooperation with the goodness and power of God represent an even higher reality than the laws of nature. Buttrick compares nature's laws to the keyboard of a piano; he compares the music to the unpredictable play of event and personality. "Obviously there are regularities: we could not live in a topsy-turvydom. But they are not the living nerve of our adventure: the nerve is the newness of inward impelling and outward event. The wonder is not in the keyboard, or even in the laws of music, but in the magic of woven sound." [12]

What is the boundary between the cosmic faithfulness of God to humanity as a whole and his willingness to alter events or circumstances in response to prayer?

> Just where the limits run who can closely trace? The land is vast and its bounds elude us. If a friend loses a hand in an accident we would not pray for a new hand to grow, but if he were sick with typhoid fever we would pray for his recovery. Where is the

boundary? We would not pray for the sun to rise in the west, but if we were caught in the track of a forest fire we might pray for the wind to change.[13]

The boundary line is often not as easy to discern as in these examples. We seldom know where the boundary is between God's cosmic faithfulness and his active presence at work in changing things in response to prayer. What should we do in such cases? Georgia Harkness gave the right answer: "If we are not sure where the limits be, the best course is to pray in humble trust and leave with God the boundaries of possibility." [14]

Does Prayer Really Change Things?

Christian faith claims that God not only helps the person praying but also uses prayer to affect persons and events beyond the person praying. Many people can understand and accept the fact that prayer changes the person who prays. However, they have difficulty believing that prayer changes things beyond the person praying. Since the latter claim—that prayer changes things—is harder to understand, let us look at it first. Then we will look at the effect of prayer on the person praying.

What exactly do Christians believe about answers to prayers calling for changes in persons, events, or circumstances? As we have seen, the claim is not that all such prayers are answered, but that some are. Many prayers are not answered. If a person chooses to, he can say that all prayers are answered: some, "yes"; some, "no"; some, "later." However, in the sense that we ask for a certain thing to happen, often it does not happen. This is the normal meaning of *answered* or *unanswered* in reference to a petitionary prayer. And in this normal usage, many prayers are unanswered.

People have prayed for sunshine and have gotten a storm; for rain, and have gotten a drought. They have prayed for doors of opportunity to open, but the doors have remained closed. They have prayed for deliverance from a bad situation, but deliverance

How Can We Believe that God Really Answers Prayers?

has not come. They have prayed for healing; yet their health has not improved. They have prayed for the life of a desperately ill person, and the person has died.

Yet this is only one side of the issue. Sometimes people have prayed for sunshine and have gotten sunshine; and for rain and have gotten rain. They have seen doors of opportunity open after they have prayed. They have sought and found deliverance from bad situations. They have prayed for and received healing. They have seen loved ones snatched from death's door after people have prayed.

Spoken and written testimonies abound of people who are strongly convinced that prayer was the crucial factor in changed lives and circumstances! Many of these testimonies—like that of Rickenbacker—tell of dramatic events that turned on prayer. Countless other people with no such dramatic testimonies are no less convinced that God has answered their prayers. In retrospect they can see many evidences to validate this faith. This kind of evidence, of course, does not prove to a skeptical mind that God answers prayer. It does validate that many people are convinced that at certain times God has definitely responded to their prayers.

Skeptics look for other ways to explain the phenomena reported as answered prayers. They prejudge the evidence by assuming that there is bound to be a purely natural explanation. They cannot always identify what the purely natural explanation of all the reported phenomena is, but they are sure that purely natural causes are at the root of the phenomena.

The other possible explanation of the phenomena is that some of the people who report answers to prayer are right. In many cases this is the most reasonable (unless one assumes that only natural explanations can ever be reasonable) explanation of the reported phenomena.

Christians believe that just as actions can change things, so can prayers. God ordained that it be so. Buttrick sums it up well: "The praying man turns the event—not always, not often, but sometimes. If he turned it always Longfellow would be right: we would govern—unto chaos. But if he turned it never, man would be a slave and God would be Coercion." [15]

Elton Trueblood makes this comment on the evidence for answered prayer:

> The reports of effective prayer are impressive. There is a deep realism in concentrating our attention, not upon what is possible or impossible, but on what *occurs* . . . . In the face of the abundant evidence of the effectiveness of prayer it is hard to dogmatize. About all that the skeptic can do is to reply that, though the result prayed for does sometimes occur, this is a mere coincidence. The solemnity of this confident answer was in one instance somewhat shaken by the humor of William Temple, when he admitted that it was conceivable that the events which occurred in his wonderful and productive life were merely coincidental, but added that the coincidences came more frequently when he prayed! [16]

The Bible teaches that God at times uses prayer to change things but he always uses prayer to help the person praying. Fosdick pointed out that God does not always answer the petition but he does always answer the person.

> This truth explains such amazing statements as Adoniram Judson, for example, made at the close of his life: "I never prayed sincerely and earnestly for anything, but it came; at some time—no matter at how distant a day—somehow, in some shape—probably the last I should have devised—it came." But Judson had prayed for entrance into India and had been compelled to go to Burma; he had prayed for his wife's life, and had buried both her and his two children; he had prayed for release from the King of Ava's prison and had lain there for months, chained and miserable. Scores of Judson's petitions had gone without an affirmative answer. But *Judson* always had been answered. He had been upheld, guided, reinforced; unforeseen doors had opened through the very trials he had sought to avoid;

and the deep desires of his life were being accomplished not in his way but beyond his way.[17]

Thus in this larger sense it is accurate to say that real prayer always is answered. The answer we seek does not always come, but the thing we need always results—and this need is met within the context of the ongoing good purpose of God. Through prayer we are brought into communion with the eternal God, our heavenly Father. We are caught up in a purpose far larger than our own plans and dreams. We are transformed according to a far better pattern than the one we would have chosen for ourselves. No wonder that the wording of the prayers of persons who persist often moves from "Give me" to "Make me" to "Show me thy glory!"

In this larger sense the prayers of Moses, David, the prophets, Paul, and Jesus were answered. Their specific requests were denied—but they and their prayers were part of the ongoing good purpose of God. For example, Paul's thorn in the flesh was not taken away; but he found a new level of commitment and trust. Jesus' cup was not taken from him. He went to the cross—but that cross became the focal point of divine redemption for sinful humanity.

Does God Need Our Prayers?

Whenever we probe the meaning of prayer, we are treading on the bounds of the mystery that is God. The biblical paradox is that although God has made himself known, he remains cloaked in mystery. If this were not so, he would no longer be God.

How then can we explain prayer? Obviously, we cannot. However, we can acknowledge its reality as well as its mystery. And we can follow what clues we have as we seek to practice it.

At the heart of the mystery is the assumption of faith that God uses our prayers to work out his will in our lives and beyond our lives. I cannot explain how he does this; but because I believe in prayer, I cannot deny it.

Sometimes the question is put like this: "If God loves us and knows our needs, why pray? Why not just trust God to meet our needs?" Jesus said that our Father knows our needs before we ask. However, Jesus did not draw from this premise the conclusion that since God knows our needs, we need not pray. To the contrary, this statement in Matthew 6:8 is immediately followed by the Lord's Prayer. The fact of God's knowledge of our needs is a basis for encouraging us to come with confident trust to God.

The truth of this matter is that God does give us many things apart from prayer, but God's best gifts require human response. "He makes his sun rise on the evil and on the good, and sends rain on the just and on the unjust" (Matt. 5:45). But God's best gifts are not automatic; they cannot be in a universe where human freedom is a God-ordained reality.

Suppose a father worked and saved in order to give his son a college education. He may discover that a college education is something he cannot *give* his son. He can make it possible financially. But the son must want it, claim it, and work for it.

Likewise, God *cannot* give us life's most precious blessings. He cannot give us such things as faith, hope, and love. He can bestow his love on us in many ways. He can seek to lead us toward the good life. But faith, hope, and love are gifts that come as we respond to God. And how do we respond? An inevitable part of the response includes prayer, for in prayer we lay our lives open to God himself.

Does God *need* our prayers? An initial impulse is to say: "No, surely not. God is God. He does not need anyone or anything. He is wholly self-sufficient in himself. His kingdom shall come and his will shall be done apart from anything we may do." There is truth in this; however, the infinite Lord of the universe has ordained that human freedom and response are the keys to the process through which he works out his will. Therefore, in this sense, God does need our prayers: He has made himself in some ways dependent on our response. There are some things that he wants to do in us and through us, but these things await our prayers. If we ask why this is so, we can only answer, "Because this is the way God has chosen to work—in a way that builds human freedom and response into the very fabric of his purpose."

Take the matter of intercessory prayer. Many people will accept the premise that God makes our neighbor's good somewhat dependent on our actions. We can deprive him of some of the good he needs by our own inaction. This is easier to accept than to believe that our neighbor's good also depends somewhat on our prayers. Yet this is the inevitable assumption of the Christian view of intercessory prayer.

There is an interdependence among the members of the body of humanity. God has made us so. Our individual freedom to act and pray is built into the fabric of our mutual interdependence.

Based on this common bond, George A. Buttrick uses an analogy or parable to try to show how intercession works. When a person has an infection, the physician may use an injection of antibiotic. The injection is made into a healthy part of the body, not directly into the infected area. However, the serum spreads its healing benefits until it attacks the infection itself. Likewise, intercessory prayer is like an injection into the common life of humanity. God causes it to spread in such a way as to attack the areas of disease. The end result is health.[18]

Man's Faith and God's Will

Buttrick's analogy assumes that God, not the person praying, takes the intercession and uses it for the best good. God and his will are always the key factors in answers to prayer. Although God uses our prayers (or to state it most strongly *needs* our prayers), God himself determines whether the prayer will be answered and, if so, how it will be answered.

The faith of the person praying is also an important factor in real prayer; however, true faith always balances confidence in God's power to answer prayer with trust that the *whether* and the *how* of prayer must be left in God's hands.

Some people emphasize the confidence element in faith almost to the exclusion of trust. They quote verses such as "Whatever you ask in prayer, you will receive, if you have faith" (Matt. 21:22). However, they fail to take note of those Bible passages that condition prayer in the will of God: "And this is the confidence which we have in him, that if we ask anything according to his will he hears us" (1 John 5:14).

Faith always must operate in the awareness that God has not only the power to answer prayer but also the wisdom and love to know when and how it should be answered. The highest faith thus combines confidence and trust. Which requires the greater faith? To believe God will answer a prayer or to trust God even when a request is denied? Both are important. Thus the spirit of Jesus' prayer in Gethesemane—"not my will, but thine be done" (Luke 22:42)—is inherent in every prayer of faith. We, of course, should beware letting this be an excuse for not expecting God to answer specific requests. However, confidence in God's power and trust in his wisdom and love are both essential to the prayer of faith.

Faith is essential in prayer, but fortunately God does not demand perfect faith. God responds to believing prayer, but he is able to do more than we dare to believe. Paul was aware of this. In Ephesians 3:14–19 he prayed one of the most comprehensive intercessory prayers ever recorded. He prayed to the limit of his faith and love; then he committed the prayer to "Him who by the power at work within us is able to do far more abundantly than all that we ask or think" (Eph. 3:20).

This should encourage us to pray—even when our faith is weak, even when it is almost nonexistent (see the end of chap. 1). The proof of prayer is in the practice of it. "The only proof of prayer is—prayer. We can no more prove prayer by argument than we can prove swimming by diagrams on shore." [19]

There is always an element of risk in faith. No one can absolutely *prove* that God is there and, if he is, that he will hear and answer our prayers. Therefore, a person can play it safe (or what seems safe from any demand for scientific proof and intellectual certainty) and never take the risk.

Or he can take the plunge and find out for himself. Buttrick tells of the man who prayed, "O God, if there be a God, save my soul, if I be a soul." [20] This may not be much of a prayer, but it is at least a start. Some who started with this little faith have been able to find enough confirmation to venture further in their pilgrimage of faith. They have found by experience the most convincing of all kinds of evidence that God really does answer prayer.

6
How Can We Believe in Life After Death?

John Killinger has an interesting essay on "Death and Transcendence in Contemporary Literature." He calls attention to the striking contrast between authors who reflect a Christian view of death and those who do not. Many twentieth-century writers reflect a complete absence of Christian hope. "Modern protagonists do not necessarily fear death; but neither do they approach it with belief in judgment and the afterlife. Many of them are in fact prepared for annihilation and do not expect to survive the first wave of unconsciousness crossing the seawall of life." [1]

Killinger traces three schools of thought on death in twentieth-century secular writers. Many writers early in the century expressed a kind of literary naturalism. Authors like Zola and Dreiser were fascinated by the gruesome reality of death as a fact of human existence. The second school, which reflected the influence of existential philosophy, predominated from World War I to mid-century. Writers like Hemingway and Camus believed that although humans are doomed to live and die in a meaningless universe, they nonetheless can face death with courage. More recent writers like Beckett and Ionesco represent the theater of the absurd. Their characters face the absurdity of life and death with helpless, absurd acts of their own.

One theme runs through all these contemporary secular schools of thought on death: Death is annihilation! The Christian hope of life after death is seldom if ever mentioned, and then not as a possibility.

The situation of the absence of hope of life after death is very much like the hopelessness that pervaded the ancient world before Christ came. Paul described the people of the Greco-Roman world as "having no hope and without God in the world" (Eph. 2:12). The writings and grave markers from the centuries just before Christ reflect a sort of hopeless despair. There were some exceptions: Some based their hope on the reasonings of philosophers like Plato, and others embraced the hopes offered by the mystery religions. However, the general mood was one of dark despair.

A central part of the good news preached by the early Christians was the hope of eternal life. They declared that the eternal purpose of God was "manifested through . . . our Savior Christ Jesus, who abolished death and brought life and immortality to light through the gospel" (2 Tim. 1:10). The people of the ancient world were not so much attracted by a superior way of living as by the promise of victory over death and entry into a life that is abundant and eternal.

The Christian view prevailed and continued until modern times. For centuries the dominant view was the certainty of life after death through Christ. We can look back on those days and criticize the people for sometimes being too morbid and sometimes too otherworldly. But it is impossible to deny their basic confidence of a life after death.

However, western civilization now has come full circle back to the absence of hope, which was characteristic before Christ came.

The Modern Skeptical Mood

What caused this widespread modern skepticism about life after death? A combination of factors—but basically the impact of science on views about God, the universe, and human life. The emergence of modern science coincided with a decline in religious beliefs. Naturalism, which many adopted as the inevitable outlook of science, denied any reality beyond what could be investigated and verified using the tools of science. This approach automatically excluded religious beliefs and undercut the kind of evidence and authority on which such beliefs are based.

The nineteenth-century British scientist Thomas Huxley exemplified the kind of outlook that excludes religious authority and beliefs. Huxley's son Noel died suddenly of scarlet fever. Huxley and his wife grieved deeply. Charles Kingsley, a clergyman, wrote Huxley and told him to claim the consolation of Christian hope. Huxley replied that the Christian belief in life after death offers enormous comfort for bereaved persons. However, Huxley said that he could not claim such a belief because it would sacrifice his fidelity to truth, which he treasured more than any amount of consolation. He felt that "truth" can be verified by the tools of science and since life after death cannot be verified in this way, it lies outside the area of known truth.

Science also brought a new view of the universe and a revised estimation of humanity's place in that universe. Beliefs about life after death assume that human beings are important enough to have continued life. The earth and humanity were central in earlier prescientific views of the universe. Science has shown that the sun does not revolve around the earth but vice versa. Also, astronomy has found that our solar system occupies only a remote corner of one of countless galaxies in a vast universe. Naturalism further compounded this cosmic insignificance of human life by assuming a machinelike universe in which human life is a purely natural phenomenon.

Science dealt another crushing blow to belief in life after death by its studies in the sciences dealing with human beings. Anthropology, physiology, biology, psychology, sociology, and medicine study humanity—individually and collectively. None of these has been able to discover a soul or spirit that survives physical death. Naturalists then draw what seems to them a logical conclusion: A person's mind or personality is only a physical function of the brain; therefore, the person perishes in every way at death.

One of the many recent books on death includes this paragraph in its introduction:

> Long and complicated discussions of the religious significance of death, and the afterlife, have not been included. These are questions each person must resolve for himself. Is there a soul, or isn't there? How many angels can dance on the head of a pin? Dozens of writers, each more astute than I, have discussed these questions. Their works are the classics of theology and philosophy.[2]

What a devastating put-down of the religious concern about life after death! Some theologians in medieval times did discuss such inane subjects as the number of angels that could get on the head of a pin, but this is hardly a burning issue for religious people. Yet this inane question is placed in the same category as the question "Is there a soul, or isn't there?" The writer's attitude seems to reflect the modern view that the whole discussion of life after death is foolish and irrelevant.

Secular Hopes of Mortal Immortality

The prevailing mood of skepticism is so strong that many people have set about to find secular alternatives for religious hope of life after death. Look at the books on death or immortality on library shelves. There is a distinct difference between more recent books and books of earlier generations. Older works on immortality, for example, usually dealt with life after death. More recent books deal with secular hopes of achieving some sort of mortal immortality.

The Prospect of Immortality by Robert C. W. Ettinger is such a book. Ettinger is a fervent evangelist for the cryonic movement. He believes that people should be frozen when they die. His boundless faith in science assumes the following: (1) Someday science will perfect a way of reviving the frozen dead. (2) By that time science also will have conquered illness and the process of aging, so that for all intents and purposes human life will be immortal. (3) By that time science also will have changed human behavior so that the revived dead will enter a totally new kind of human society.

Here is Ettinger's glowing prophecy of what awaits a person who seeks immortality through refrigeration:

> After awakening, he may already be again young and virile, having been rejuvenated while unconscious; or he may be gradually renovated through treatment after awakening. In any case, he will have the physique of a Charles Atlas if he wants it, and his weary and faded wife, if she chooses, may rival Miss America. Much more important, they will be gradually improved in mentality and personality . . . .
>
> If civilization endures, if the Golden Age materializes, the future will reveal a wonderful world indeed . . . . The key difference will be in *people*; we will remold, nearer to the heart's desire, not just the world, but ourselves as well. You and I, the frozen, the resuscitees, will be not merely revived and cured, but enlarged and improved, made fit to work, play, and perhaps fight on a grand scale and in a grand style.[3]

Osborn Segerberg, Jr. investigates a more limited approach to the secular hope of mortal immortality. In his book *The Immortality Factor* he concentrates on the possibilities and implications of conquering the aging process. Segerberg concedes that parapsychology may someday provide scientific evidence for survival beyond death. However, he believes that many modern-day people want no immortality that does not include the sensual experiences of present mortal existence. He refers to Ettinger's book and to the cryonics movement as being based on untested and unproved hopes and assumptions. However, he is optimistic about the possibilities of attaining mortal immortality by conquering aging: "The fountain of youth exists. Fruit still grows on the tree of life. Paradise is not lost. We can return to Eden, theoretically. Achieving the goal, like going to the moon, becomes a problem for technology." [4]

However, Segerberg is not so optimistic about society's ability to solve the problems that will arise in implementing a technology capable of making an ageless society. He observes that advances in scientific technology do not guarantee favorable long-range outcomes: "The promise, the commitment of biological gerontology is to make the phrase 'and they lived happily ever after' come true. However, molecular biologists cannot be expected to guarantee the happiness part. Their training qualifies them only for 'and they lived ever after,' which is another state of affairs." [5] Segerberg's advice, therefore, is that specialists from many disciplines need to be involved in deciding what course society should take with regard to implementing mortal immortality.

Both Ettinger and Segerberg discuss hopes of mortal immortality based on the conquest of aging and death. There are other kinds of secular immortality that are not based on an actual conquest of death. Some people face death armed with what is sometimes called biological immortality. These people expect no actual personal survival after death, but they expect to achieve a sort of immortality through the continued existence of their children, grandchildren, and later descendants.

Social or cultural immortality is similar in many ways: A person lives in such a way that he hopes to be remembered by generations after his death. Thus he is immortalized in the memory of succeeding generations.

Carliss Lamont in his book *The Illusion of Immortality* rejected any hope of personal immortality, but he did say that " 'we can make our actions count and endow our days on earth with a scope and meaning that the finality of death cannot defeat.'" Jacques Choron quotes Lamont and then makes this judgment about such hopes: "Although we can make our existence 'full,' 'successful,' and 'meaningful' we cannot give it any meaning that death, if it is final annihilation, would not destroy. And although we can devote our life to 'humanity,' humanity itself is perishable." [6]

What Is "Life After Death"?

One basic flaw in biological immortality and social immortality is that neither is personal. The traditional understanding of life after death, at least in Western culture, has been personal survival of death. The essence of the real person—whether called soul, spirit, personality, or mind—survives death. The body and the brain die, but the person does not.

The philosopher Charles Hartshorne suggests a view of immortality by which our lives are recorded in the knowledge and memory of an eternal God. This avoids the obvious flaw of social immortality: Few of us are remembered for very long by the human race, and none of us will be remembered when the human race ends. However, Hartshorne's view falls short of the traditional Christian view of *personal* life after death.

This personal aspect is one of the central features of the Christian belief in life after death. The Christian doctrine of resurrection does not mean a resuscitation of the physical body but a redemption of the total personality. Jesus did not agree with the skeptical Sadducees who denied life after death; nor did he teach the extremely literal resurrection of the Pharisees. He taught that the life beyond is a different mode of being (see Matt. 22:23-33). Paul's description of the spiritual body is the most detailed biblical discussion of life beyond death (see 1 Cor. 15:35-50). Paul made no attempt to give details of the life beyond. He left many questions unanswered. However, what he did say clearly affirms that life after death is personal.

How Can We Believe in Life After Death?

This view is in striking contrast not only to those who deny any kind of real life after death but also to those who teach a sort of impersonal immortality. For example, Buddhism hopes for an escape from endless existence into nirvana. In Buddhist thought reincarnation is not a happy prospect (as it is in the minds of most Westerners who grasp it as a hope). The soul is reincarnated in a cycle of rebirths, into an existence filled with suffering and misery. The Buddhist seeks a detached state of mind that is oblivious to earthly existence. The hope is that this will break the cycle of rebirths and enable the soul to be extinguished into nirvana, the ultimate state of detachment.

The whole system is an attempt to escape all those marks of personality—individuality, self-consciousness, identity. By contrast, the Christian view of life after death affirms these marks of personality.

Quality is another closely related aspect of the Christian view of life after death. The emphasis in the biblical term *eternal life* is quality, not quantity. Eternal life is everlasting, but what makes it appealing is that it is *life*. What is offered is not endless existence after death but life after death. If the choice were between annihilation at death or endless existence after death, most discerning people would prefer annihilation.

Life is a key biblical word. Christ is the bearer of life that is abundant and eternal. The early Christians did not make the mistake of some later generations of believers. The early Christians did not seek to fill in the details of the afterlife. They were content not to know the answers to questions about what it would be like. They were content to affirm the certainty and desirability of eternal life.

The Christian hope is an unapologetically religious hope, rooted in God's gracious purpose. In biblical terms it is a resurrection hope. This hope has some affinities with Plato's philosophy of immortality of the soul. However, there also are some striking differences. Resurrection is a miracle by which God gives life to the dead; immortality implies that men are by nature immortal. Some philosophers build a view of immortality without God, but no one can conceive of resurrection without God.

The ancient Greeks were no less scientific than people today in this respect: Both agree that dead bodies do not come back to life. The doctrine of resurrection is open to ridicule when it is interpreted as a restoration to life of our flesh-and-blood bodies. The biblical idea of resurrection was given to show the Christian hope as centered in God's grace, power, and purpose; it was not a claim that the future resurrection will be on biological terms.

Plato and those who have followed him tend to emphasize the individual's survival of death. The Bible doctrine of resurrection focuses not on the death of each believer but on the consummation of God's purpose for all his people. Individual personality is part of this, but the Bible always defines personality in the context of God and others. Thus the spotlight is not on me and whether or not I will survive death; it is on God and whether or not his purpose will be achieved.

Is There Any Scientific Evidence for Life After Death?

What is the basis for hope of life after death? The discussion includes three domains: science, philosophy, and religion. (1) What, if any, is the scientific evidence for life after death? (2) What philosophical arguments can be used to support it? (3) What are the religious reasons for the Christian hope of life after death?

Spiritualism purports to give evidence of survival beyond death. Some people have dabbled in it as a kind of game. Others have turned to it in grief, seeking some contact with a departed loved one. Some people believe it, but most are skeptical. One reason for skepticism is the number of hoaxes that have been uncovered. Another reason is the nature of the supposed "communications." Few if any remarkable insights are reported. Elton Trueblood

How Can We Believe in Life After Death?

quotes with approval this judgment of A. E. Taylor from his book *The Faith of a Moralist.* Taylor says that the alleged messages "are mostly a medley of sentimental gush and twaddling sermonizing." [7]

Parapsychology is a relatively new branch of science that studies psychic phenomena of all kinds. Parapsychologists hope to learn if there is any empirical evidence for survival after death. Thus far they have found some intriguing clues, some baffling puzzles, but no empirical evidence.

Many readers of Raymond A. Moody's book *Life After Life* are convinced that he has compiled empirical evidence for life after death. He obviously has compiled data about phenomena that parapsychologists and others need to give attention to. Moody interviewed about fifty people who had unusual experiences either after they had been pronounced clinically dead or when they had come very close to dying. These people were interviewed separately and apart from any awareness of what others were saying. Yet all reported a continuing state of existence and awareness.

Moody found a basic agreement among these reports. He identified fifteen separate elements that recurred in the narratives he collected. No person reported all fifteen; but each element showed up in many stories, a few elements were in almost every story, and a large number of elements appeared in many accounts.[8]

One of the most striking elements was a kind of "out of the body" experience. Many of the persons who had died saw their own dead bodies. Several watched efforts to revive them. Some later reported to their doctors things that were said and done after they were dead.

Moody examines a number of possible natural explanations for these reports. He does not believe that any of these explanations adequately explain the phenomena reported to him. Moody himself refuses to draw any conclusions. He denies that his studies have proved life after death. However, he does not rule this out as a possible explanation. He considers these reports as significant enough for further study: "I think that these reports are very significant. What I want to do is to find some middle way of interpreting them—a way which neither rejects these experiences on the basis that they do not constitute scientific or logical proof nor sensationalizes them by resorting to vague emotional claims that they 'prove' that there is life after death." [9]

Those of us who believe in life after death should avoid drawing unwarranted conclusions from the kind of phenomena reported by Moody. We cannot help being intrigued by the whole field of parapsychology. We need not be anxious about what science may or may not discover. The Christian view of life after death never has been and never will be dependent on empirical scientific evidence. We can hope that one result of such studies may be a broader definition of what constitutes or may constitute reality.

What Are the Philosophical Arguments for Life After Death?

Since ancient times, philosophers have argued about the possibility of life after death. Not surprisingly, a philosopher's conclusions about life after death are largely determined by his basic premises and presuppositions. As we have seen, these are the premises that lead to a denial of life after death: (1) The only reality is natural. (2) The universe is devoid of mind or purpose. (3) Human personality is a purely physical attribute of the body and brain. Those who affirm the possibility of life after death on philosophical grounds begin with the opposite premises.

Neither side can prove its case or exclude the other possibility on scientific or philosophical grounds. Each can only attack the premises of the other side and seek to set forth its own premises in a convincing way.

How Can We Believe in Life After Death?

The battle is joined over the question "What is truth or reality?" This was the crucial question in earlier chapters, when we examined such subjects as God, miracles, and prayer. This is also the crucial question in dealing with philosophical arguments about life after death. Christians challenge the naturalists' assumption that their definition of truth is broad enough to include all reality.

Harry Emerson Fosdick used the analogy of an unborn child in the womb. Based on his experience, the child cannot conceive of the possibility of surviving the impending crisis of birth:

> He lives without air; how can he live with it? He never saw light; how can he conceive of it? He is absolutely dependent upon the cherishing environment in which he finds himself, and he cannot well imagine himself living without it. The crisis of birth would seem like death to an unborn child, if he could foresee himself wrenched from all the conditions which have hitherto sustained his life.[10]

Fosdick's analogy does not prove anything, but it is an attempt to show that what is real may be larger than what our present knowledge and experience can confirm as truth.

In a later writing Fosdick enlarged on his analogy. Fosdick imagined twins in their mother's womb. He imagined that they could think and talk to one another. They discuss the possibility of life beyond the womb. One is skeptical, but the other is a believer. The skeptic challenges his twin to explain how he can believe in life beyond the womb. The believer replies: "Month after month nature has been at work here developing something so marvelous that I am confident of an aftermath . . . . Nature is not so senseless as to undertake such a promising process with no end in view. The crisis that you call death will turn out really to be birth." [11]

Again Fosdick's analogy proves nothing, but it does illustrate one of the philosophical arguments used to support the possibility of life after death—the argument that purpose in the universe leads to the need for life after death.

The question about mind and purpose in the universe is a focal point of philosophical arguments about life after death. Those who assume a purposeful universe tend to conclude that life after death is possible if not probable. It is impossible of course if, as naturalists claim, human life is only an obscure, purely natural phenomenon in a remote part of a vast, uncaring universe. However, if human personality is part of a creative process, life after death is needed for further development.

Who has not felt the sense of incompleteness that accompanies the news of someone's death? This feeling is especially acute if the person was young. However, there is a sense in which the feeling is there when an elderly person dies, especially if we know the person well. The feeling of incompleteness is there for many people when they try to contemplate their own death. Viewed from the perspective of the years, we seem hardly to have begun life when the curtain falls. Victor Hugo at the age of seventy wrote: "Winter is on my head, but spring is in my heart. For half a century I have been writing, but I have not said a thousandth part of what is in me."

The philosopher Immanuel Kant proposed a moral argument for immortality. He assumed progress in morality as a part of the purpose for human personality. If human beings are designed to seek moral ends, the destruction of human personality would thwart the attaining of that goal. Therefore, Kant concluded, we need eternity to fulfill our intended moral growth.

A similar point is made when human personality is described in terms of the need for ultimate meaning. Not everyone agrees that ultimate meaning is essential, but those who do have taken a giant step toward a strong philosophical basis for life after death. Jacques Choron probes the relation between ultimate meaning and life after death in his book *Death and Modern Man*. Logically, the person who denies one of these is almost driven to deny the other;

likewise, affirming one involves affirming the other. If human personality is annihilated at death, many people have trouble avoiding the conclusion that life makes no sense. This does not prove the survival of personality, but it does explain why many modern people see life and death as meaningless, even absurd. "Death may be 'nothing' as Epicurus and some modern, 'tough-minded' philosophers claim, for it is 'only' a natural end of life; but it, nevertheless, turns life into 'nothing' by making it appear pointless and absurd, a journey whose final destination is disaster, a struggle that is fated to be lost." [12]

At the heart of philosophical arguments about life after death are questions about human personality: Is the mind or personality purely a function of the brain, or is mind a larger reality than the brain? The mind and personality of living persons are obviously linked with the functions of the body and brain. Naturalists insist that the mind is purely a function of the brain and, therefore, at death when the brain perishes, so does the mind and personality. By contrast others claim that the essential being of the person—whatever it is called—survives death. Philosophers who defend this concept seek to show that human personality is more than a function of the brain.

A sense of self-consciousness and personal identity seems to support this point of view. This is especially true when this awareness of oneself is contrasted with the continuing physical changes in the body and brain. As a person grows and ages, body cells, including brain cells, are constantly dying and being replaced. Yet a person's awareness of himself survives all of these changes intact.

J. Paterson Smyth develops this argument in his book *The Gospel of the Hereafter*. He refers to the mysterious self-conscious "I" of human personality. This conscious personality is related closely to the functions of the brain, but it is more than the brain. Smyth pictures a medical student looking at a human brain on a dissecting table. He knows the arguments pro and con, but as he looks at the exposed human brain, "Something within him indignantly replies: Nay 'I' am not the brain. I possess it. I use it. 'It is mine, but it is not I!' " [13]

As a Christian philosopher, Elton Trueblood has puzzled over this complex and highly debatable issue of the relationship of self-consciousness and the brain. How can the consciousness continue without the brain? Trueblood writes:

> The problem has not ceased to worry me, but I have been helped, immeasurably, by the consideration of a companion problem. How can it be that, in a world made up basically of merely material forces, there would even arise a being who is puzzled by the very fact of his being. I saw that here was a mystery, not less great, but even greater than that of the continuation of personal identity after the decay of brain tissue. But the overwhelming fact is that the step from matter to self-consciousness *has already been taken* . . . . However great, then, may be the miracle of survival, it is more than matched by the known and already enacted miracle of arrival. [14]

What Are the Religious Reasons?

Although the philosophical arguments for life after death have some value, they have little persuasiveness apart from some religious faith. Philosophers can and sometimes do argue both sides of the question of the possibility of life after death. Without religious faith the philosophical arguments are at best inconclusive.

Not everyone who believes in God also believes in life after death, but faith in the God described in the Bible gives strong reasons for believing in life after death. In the early stages of the Old Testament the Hebrew people had little concept of life after death. They assumed some sort of survival beyond death, but this was not something they anticipated with any relish. However, as the people grew in their experience with a God of love and justice,

How Can We Believe in Life After Death?

they began to probe the possibility of some kind of meaningful life beyond the grave. Job, for example, struggled with the seeming injustice of his terrible sufferings. The prevailing view of his day assumed that justice is dispensed adequately in this life. Job's experience forced him to deny this assumption. His experience led him to begin to move wistfully toward the possibility of life after death.

The people of Old Testament times moved wistfully toward life after death also because they were increasingly convinced of God's purpose for his people. God was doing something significant in and among them. This "something" he was doing had a transcendence far beyond earthly movements and plans. God's purpose stretched over the generations and into the ages to come.

This conviction about God's purpose was blended with a growing conviction of God's gracious concern for his people—individually and collectively. These were the first roots of the hope of future resurrection. If God loves a person, will he limit that person's sharing in God's purpose to the brief span of earthly life? Will only one future generation share the joy of the consummation of God's purpose? As the years passed, more and more of the Hebrew people were answering no to these questions.

Yet hope in the Old Testament was more a wistful longing than a confident belief. All of this was changed for those who followed Jesus Christ after his resurrection from the dead. The exultant confidence of Christian hope is well expressed by Peter: "Blessed be the God and Father of our Lord Jesus Christ! By his great mercy we have been born anew to a living hope through the resurrection of Jesus Christ from the dead" (1 Pet. 1:3).

Chapter 3 gives the reasons Christians believe in the resurrection of Christ. These will not be repeated here. The point here is that faith in the risen Christ is the key factor in our hope of life after death. For centuries men had feared death as the end. After all, they had said, no one has ever come back to tell us otherwise. Now one had come back—not just anyone, but the Son of God. And he came back not just as one restored to life again; rather, he came back as the conqueror of death. He did not return to tell details of the afterlife; rather, he came announcing the death of death and the certainty of eternal life for those who claim his promise.

The resurrection of Christ means more than the assurance of eternal life, but it surely includes this assurance. Paul based the whole Christian enterprise on the reality of Christ's resurrection. At stake is the truth of the gospel message, the forgiveness of our sins, and the hope of life after death. If Christ was not raised from the dead, none of these is true. But because he has been raised, all of these things and many more are true (see 1 Cor. 15:12–19).

One of the charges made against hope of life after death is that this is only an illusion based on what we wish were so. This is the same kind of logic that assumes that faith in God as Father is based only on a wish for a powerful father-figure. As we noted in chapter 4, this accusation fits some but not all of the data. There is enough truth in it to make it sound plausible, but it does not explain why men would invent a God who calls his followers to the way of the cross.

Is life after death only an illusion based on what people wish were so? This charge would be more convincing if Christian hope were only a tentative conclusion at the end of a series of philosophical arguments. Christian hope is part of the total Christian commitment which includes the cross as well as the resurrection.

This much at least is true of the charge that hope is only a wish: Christian hope is a very attractive concept, particularly when contrasted with the alternatives. Christian hope was a key factor in helping the early believers outlive and outdie the pagan world. Christian hope is not some irrelevant, otherworldly speculation. Eternal life begins in the here and now, and it pervades all of a person's attitudes and actions.

Chapter 4 described the Christian life in terms of three qualities that are needed by all people but found most fully in Christ—forgiveness, meaning, and hope. These are the qualities of the way of life for those who follow the crucified-risen Jesus Christ. How preferable this life is to an existence without God and without hope!

Some people in the latter category deny that theirs is a bleak existence. They claim to feel no need for divine forgiveness. They are able to find meaning enough without resorting to religion. They can face death without religious hope. Some even claim that a belief in annihilation better equips a person for enjoying life and for facing death. The assumption is that since a person knows this life is all there is, he will live each day to the fullest. And when he faces death, he can accept the end with calm resignation.

Yet how rich and full can be a life that runs into a dead end? Such a person can find meanings in various experiences of life, but how can he find any overall meaning to life? No doubt some are able to find something akin to this by being caught up in some great movement that they feel will extend far beyond their lifetime. And others may go through life seldom if ever wondering about any ultimate meaning to their lives. But neither group has the solid base for meaningful living provided by Christian faith and hope.

And what about the fear of death and the experience of dying? The fear of death is a kind of primal instinct. People fear death for many reasons. They fear the process of dying. They fear what may happen after death. They fear that death is the end and that they therefore will cease to be. Fear can seldom be coped with purely on the conscious, rational level. No doubt some people who believe death is the end face dying with courage and dignity. Many people, however, including some who lack Christian hope, concede that the Christian belief in life after death is the best antidote for the fear of death and the best basic equipment for coping with the actual process of dying. Indeed, this assumption is the basis for the charge that life after death is only wishful thinking.

Wistful Wish or Wise Wager?

Some non-Christians reject Christian hope precisely because it is so attractive. Like Thomas Huxley, they are prisoners of their own definition of truth. Huxley would not compromise the "truth" in order to claim the comfort of Christian hope.

Jacques Choron's book *Death and Modern Man* reveals the author's own quest for some answer about life after death. But he seeks assurance based on philosophical arguments, not religious faith. He explains: "There is here no intention of militating against the religious outlook and all those who can find their way to it ought to be envied and congratulated. But one must be aware of the difficulties of many because the 'leap of faith' seems to be not to everyone's taste or within one's capability." [15]

He presents philosophical arguments on both sides of the issue. He especially builds a strong case for the possibility of continued life because of the need for ultimate meaning. At times he seems on the verge of making a philosophical decision in favor of life after death. He obviously wants to believe in life after death. He wants to be persuaded that this is possible, even probable. However, each time he is almost persuaded, he backs away—for fear that his personal preference for this view will influence his decision.

Blaise Pascal's famous analogy of the wager suggests that the very desirability of this option should encourage rather than discourage one to commit himself in this direction. Pascal, one of the leading scientists of his day and a committed Christian, suggested this analogy as a way of helping unbelievers who are wistful about Christianity but who claim to be unable to believe.

In a dialogue with an imaginary unbeliever Pascal suggested that the person's option to believe or not to believe is like a person betting on whether or not a coin will be heads or tails. Pascal did not believe that science or religion could either prove or disprove God. Therefore, because he can neither prove nor disprove God, the person must move into the area of faith. He has two choices: He can either believe or he can refuse to believe. Thus in a sense he must gamble his life either that God is or that he is not. The nature of this game is such that a person cannot evade making some decision—one way or the other.

Therefore, faced with the necessity of wagering, the person must decide whether to stake all on "God is, or He is not." Pascal's advice is clear: "Let us weigh the gain and the loss in wagering that God is. Let us estimate these two chances. If you gain, you gain all; if you lose you lose nothing. Wager, then, without hesitation." [16]

Pascal's point is that the person who gambles his life on God stands either to gain or to lose "an eternity of life and happiness." Thus, if he is right and God is real, he has gained everything. But suppose he later finds he was wrong. What has he lost? Nothing. If he gambles on God and later finds he was wrong, he is only back where he was to start with—without "an eternity of life and happiness." However, if he refuses to stake his life on God, the results are clear: He foregoes any chance at abundant and eternal life.

Pascal's imaginary seeker admits the force of his arguments, but he pleads (as do many modern unbelievers) that he is so made that he cannot believe. Pascal then challenges the unbeliever to embark on the pilgrimage of faith by beginning to act "as if" he believed.

This advice probably strikes many modern readers as a call to be guilty of hypocrisy: "First he asks me to bet my life that God is real when I have no way of knowing. Then he tells me to do this by acting as if I believed that God is real!"

But ask yourself whether or not you have been able either to prove or disprove Christianity. Why then wait around for proof from science or philosophy? Such proof will never come. The issue must be decided some other way.

What other way? By faith! And what is faith? Faith is not seeing the end of the way at the beginning. It is putting one foot before the other and taking the first step in the pilgrimage of faith. Often the first step is praying to a God you are not even sure is there to hear.

For most believers there is a growing certitude as one moves on in the Christian pilgrimage. There are times of light and of darkness. The light tends to bring assurance that our commitment is based on something real. The darkness tends to bring doubt and uncertainty because we still walk by faith, not sight. There is a sense in which the entire Christian pilgrimage is living one's life "as if" God is, but at no time is this so true than in taking the first step of faith and commitment.

After all, Pascal was right on both counts: (1) You have everything to gain and nothing to lose by such a commitment. (2) You will never know whether or not it is real until you have tried it for yourself. As the psalmist said: "Taste and see that the Lord is good!" (Ps. 34:8.)

Notes

Introduction

1. Elton Trueblood, *A Place to Stand* (New York: Harper and Row, 1969), pp. 17–21.

Chapter 1

1. See William Hordern, *Speaking of God: the Nature and Purpose of Theological Language* (New York: The Macmillan Company, 1964).
2. Eric C. Rust, *Science and Faith* (New York: Oxford University Press, 1967), p. 61.
3. Elton Trueblood, *Philosophy of Religion* (New York: Harper and Brothers, 1957), p. 196.
4. Ibid., p. 75.
5. George Arthur Buttrick, *The Christian Fact and Modern Doubt* (New York: Charles Scribner's Sons, 1934), p. 26.
6. Quoted by James C. Hefley, *Lift-off!* (Grand Rapids: Zondervan Publishing Company, 1970), p. 24.
7. William Temple, *Nature, Man and God* (London: Macmillan and Company, Limited, 1953), p. 133.
8. Rust, p. 63.
9. Trueblood, *Philosophy of Religion*, p. 97.
10. Buttrick, p. 8.
11. Trueblood, *Philosophy of Religion*, p. 109.

12. Ibid., pp. 113–114.

13. Ibid., p. 117.

14. C. S. Lewis, *Mere Christianity* (New York: The Macmillan Company, 1958), p. 31.

15. Trueblood, *Philosophy of Religion*, pp. 143–158.

16. Ibid., p. 73.

17. Leslie D. Weatherhead, *Key Next Door* (New York: Abingdon Press, 1960), p. 140.

18. See Eric C. Rust, *Toward a Theological Understanding of History* (New York: Oxford University Press, 1963), pp. 12–16.

19. George A. Buttrick, *Prayer* (New York: Abingdon Press, 1942), pp. 68–69.

CHAPTER 2

1. Leonard Griffith, *God's Time and Ours* (New York: Abingdon Press, 1964), p. 47.

2. R. Lofton Hudson, *The Religion of a Sound Mind* (Nashville: Broadman Press, 1949), p. 19.

3. George A. Buttrick, *God, Pain, and Evil* (New York: Abingdon Press, 1966), p. 19.

4. Archibald MacLeish, *J. B.* (New York: Samuel French, Inc., 1956), p. 18.

5. Elton Trueblood, *Philosophy of Religion* (New York: Harper and Brothers, 1957), p. 231.

6. C. S. Lewis, *The Problem of Pain* (New York: The Macmillan Company, 1948).

7. C. S. Lewis, *A Grief Observed* (New York: The Seabury Press, 1961).

8. Thornton Wilder, *The Bridge of San Luis Rey* (New York: Time Incorporated, 1963).

9. Leslie D. Weatherhead, *The Will of God* (New York: Abingdon Press, 1944), p. 20.

10. Lewis, *The Problem of Pain*, p. 26.

11. Ibid., pp. 47–48.

12. T. B. Maston, *Suffering—a Personal Perspective* (Nashville: Broadman Press, 1967), p. 1.

13. Ibid., p. 3.

14. Trueblood, *Philosophy of Religion*, p. 239.

15. Hordern, *Speaking of God*, p. 77.

16. Buttrick, *God, Pain, and Evil*, p. 110.

17. John Claypool, *Tracks of a Fellow Struggler: How to Handle Grief* (Waco: Word Books, 1974), pp. 72–79.

18. Lewis, *A Grief Observed*, pp. 54–55.

19. Ibid., p. 60.

CHAPTER 3

1. Malcolm Muggeridge, *Jesus Rediscovered* (Wheaton: Tyndale House Publishers, 1969), p. 58.

2. Ibid., pp. 166–167.

3. Leonard Griffith, *Barriers to Christian Belief* (New York: Harper and Row, 1961, 1962), p. 92.

4. D. M. Baillie, *God Was in Christ*, 2nd ed. (London: Faber and Faber Limited, 1955), p. 66.

5. C. S. Lewis, *Mere Christianity* (New York: The Macmillan Company, 1958), p. 41.

6. William Hordern, "Introduction," *New Directions in Theology Today* 1 (Philadelphia: The Westminster Press, 1966), p. 65.

7. Ibid., p. 67.

8. Alan Richardson, *Christian Apologetics* (New York: Harper and Brothers, 1947), p. 170.

9. Ibid., p. 174.

10. David Hume, "An Enquiry Concerning Human Understanding," *Great Books of the Western World* 35 (Chicago: Encyclopaedia Britannica, Inc., 1952), p. 491.

11. C. S. Lewis, *Miracles* (New York: The Macmillan Company, 1947), p. 124.

12. Ibid., p. 21.

13. Rust, *Science and Faith*, pp. 32–34.

14. Compare Ibid., p. 297.

15. Lewis, *Miracles*, p. 132.

16. George Eldon Ladd, *Why I Believe in the Resurrection of Jesus* (Grand Rapids: William B. Eerdmans Publishing Company, 1975), p. 22.

17. Hugh J. Schonfield, *The Passover Plot* (New York: Bernard Geis Associates, 1965), pp. 179–180.

18. Trueblood, *A Place to Stand*, pp. 39–40.

19. Griffith, *Barriers to Christian Belief*, p. 183.

20. John Bunyan, *The Pilgrim's Progress* (Philadelphia: The John C. Winston Company, 1933), p. 10.

Chapter 4

1. Georgia Harkness, *The Modern Rival of Christian Faith* (New York: Abingdon-Cokesbury Press, 1952), pp. 11–13.
2. Bertrand Russell, *Why I Am Not a Christian and Other Essays on Religion and Related Subjects* (New York: Simon and Schuster, 1957), p. 21.
3. G. K. Chesterton, *Orthodoxy* (New York: Dodd, Mead and Company, 1959), pp. 272–273.
4. Roger L. Shinn, *Man: the New Humanism, New Directions in Theology Today* 6 (Philadelphia: The Westminster Press, 1968), pp. 24,59.
5. Elton Trueblood, *While It Is Day* (New York: Harper and Row, 1974), pp. 68–69.
6. Buttrick, *God, Pain, and Evil*, p. 130.
7. Elton Trueblood, "Ideas that Shape the American Mind," *Christianity Today*, 6 January 1967, p. 3.
8. Weatherhead, *Key Next Door*, p. 122.
9. Karl Menninger, *Whatever Became of Sin?* (New York: Hawthorn Books, Inc., 1973), p. 46.
10. Dag Hammarskjöld, *Markings*, trans. Leif Sjöberg and W. H. Auden (New York: Alfred A. Knopf, 1964), p. v.
11. Ibid., p. 86.
12. Ibid., p. 205.
13. Viktor E. Frankl, *Man's Search for Meaning: an Introduction to Logotherapy*, trans. Ilse Lasch (Boston: Beacon Press, 1962), pp. 98–99.
14. Langdon Gilkey, *Maker of Heaven and Earth* (New York: Doubleday and Company, Inc., 1959), p. 145.
15. Karl Menninger, *The Vital Balance: the Life Process in Mental Health and Illness* (New York: The Viking Press, 1963), p. 417.
16. Buttrick, *God, Pain, and Evil*, p. 167.
17. Chesterton, p. 155.
18. Ibid., pp. 165–166.

Chapter 5

1. Griffith, *Barriers to Christian Belief*, p. 111.
2. Edward V. Rickenbacker, *Rickenbacker* (Englewood Cliffs: Prentice-Hall, Inc., 1967), p. 361.
3. Buttrick, *Prayer*, p. 15.

4. Harry Emerson Fosdick, *The Meaning of Prayer* (New York: Association Press, 1922), p. 1.

5. Lawrence M. Brings, ed., *We Believe in Prayer* (Minneapolis: T. S. Denison and Company, 1958), pp. 6–7.

6. Fosdick, p. 13.

7. Ibid., p. 133.

8. Mark Twain, *The Adventures of Huckleberry Finn* (New York: Grosset and Dunlap, 1918), p. 15.

9. Buttrick, *Prayer*, p. 65.

10. Quoted by Griffith, *Barriers to Christian Belief*, p. 114.

11. Buttrick, *Prayer*, p. 65.

12. Ibid., p. 295.

13. Ibid., p. 114.

14. Georgia Harkness, *Prayer and the Common Life* (New York: Abingdon Press, 1948), p. 70.

15. Buttrick, *Prayer*, p. 295.

16. Trueblood, *A Place to Stand*, p. 97.

17. Fosdick, *The Meaning of Prayer*, pp. 130–131.

18. Buttrick, *Prayer*, pp. 108–109.

19. Ibid., p. 154.

20. Ibid.

CHAPTER 6

1. John Killinger, *Perspective on Death*, ed. Liston O. Mills (New York: Abingdon Press, 1969), p. 138.

2. David Hendin, *Death as a Fact of Life* (New York: W. W. Norton and Company, Inc., 1973), p. 12.

3. Robert C. W. Ettinger, *The Prospect of Immortality* (Garden City, New York: Doubleday and Company, Inc., 1964), p. 6.

4. Osborn Sergerberg, Jr., *The Immortality Factor* (New York: E. P. Dutton and Company, Inc., 1974), p. 240.

5. Ibid., p. 252.

6. Jacques Choron, *Death and Modern Man* (New York: Collier Books, 1964), p. 175.

7. Quoted by Trueblood, *Philosophy of Religion*, p. 297.

8. Raymond A. Moody, Jr., *Life After Life* (New York: Bantam Books, 1975), pp. 21–25.

9. Ibid., p. 182.

10. Harry Emerson Fosdick, *The Assurance of Immortality* (New York: The Macmillan Company, 1913), pp. 55–56.

11. Harry Emerson Fosdick, *As I See Religion* (New York: Harper and Brothers, 1932), pp. 59–60.

12. Choron, p. 163.

13. J. Paterson Smyth, *The Gospel of the Hereafter* (Westwood, New Jersey: Fleming H. Revell Company, 1961), p. 24.

14. Trueblood, *A Place to Stand,* pp. 119–120.

15. Choron, p. 177.

16. Blaise Pascal, *Pensées,* section 3, 233, trans. W. F. Trotter, *Great Books of the Western World* 33 (Chicago: William Benton, 1952), p. 215.